W9-AOP-535

NATIONAL GEOGRAPHIC KiDS

125 True Stories of Amazing Animal Friendships

125 True Stories of Amazing Animal Friendships

INSPIRING TRUE STORIES OF UNEXPECTED FRIENDSHIPS, PURR-FECT PALS, AND ADORABLE BEST BUDS!

Princess Leia and Lola
Pages 16–17

NATIONAL GEOGRAPHIC KiDS

WASHINGTON, D.C.

Contents

Introduction

Ash and Archer
Page 80

GET READY to be amazed, prepare to be inspired, and practice a few *awwws* while you're at it, because you're about to read 125 of the cutest, sweetest, and most uplifting animal friendship stories ever.

Among many others, you will meet Maude, a porcupine who has been adopted by three bulldogs; Angel, a severely injured goat who found a friend and protector in a pig named Piney; and Carll, a once lonely llama who befriended a special-needs chicken who uses a wheelchair.

The paw-some stories throughout these pages include koalas, chimpanzees, horses, donkeys, geese, goats, camels, kangaroos, hedgehogs, and capybaras. The friendships range from the outrageous and hilarious to the moving and inspiring.

Sure, animals might not have the digital dexterity needed to text, and they haven't quite figured out how to drive a car, but there is one thing animals have definitely mastered—and that's friendship.

Animals have an incredible way of making it so super simple. Animals don't pick friends based on how popular they are, how much money they have, what they look like, where their parents are from, or what religion they practice. Animals seem to have only a few criteria for finding a friend: Are you kind? Are you loyal? Are you fun? Okay, then, let's be buds.

As you read the amazing stories in this book, you'll probably agree: We humans could learn a thing or two from these animals' open minds and open hearts. Enjoy!

Smudge and Ducks
Page 98

Chompers and Littlefoot
Pages 52–53

Delilah and Cherry
Page 35

MIRI AND JET

Pages 28–29

OUR FRIENDSHIP IS FIN-TASTIC!

DOG GROOMS FAWN

LOCATION: MOORELAND, OKLAHOMA, U.S.A.

Get ready for the cutest story of all time. When a little fawn named Baby lost his mother, he had no one to take care of him. Thankfully, Miranda and Don Stidham took Baby in and began nursing him back to health. He now not only gets two big bottles of milk a day, he also gets an amazing caretaker in the form of the Stidhams' dog, Coop. The two adore each other, and everywhere that Coop goes, Baby is close behind. They love to run and play and chase each other. But during those epic play sessions outside in the yard, Baby sometimes accumulates lots of burrs in his coat. So, amazingly, every morning and every evening, the sweet, doting dog will pick the burrs off of Baby with his mouth. Grooming, for animals, is an act of love—and these two cuties have loads of it to give. Baby couldn't ask for a better caretaker!

PIT BULL PUP BECOMES HEN'S BEST FRIEND

LOCATION: LOS ANGELES, CALIFORNIA, U.S.A.

This unlikely love story began when Crystalyn and her husband, Damon, decided to adopt a chicken. They rescued Rosie and her sister Daisy from a farm where the hens had been neglected and overworked. Now the two hens were able to roam freely outside for the first time in their lives! Sadly, a few years later, Daisy got very sick and passed away. Crystalyn and Damon worried that Rosie should have a companion, but any time another animal came to the house, the little hen would act, well, chicken! But then Crystalyn and Damon found out about a pit bull who was very sick and in desperate need of care. They decided to help her, but they knew they could keep her only if they could be sure she wouldn't hurt Rosie. So, very carefully, they introduced Rosie and the pup, whom they named Maggie. This time, Rosie didn't squawk and she didn't run away! From then on, the two have been great friends. Rosie eats the peas out of Maggie's food bowl and Maggie happily lets her. They sleep near each other, and every morning Maggie licks Rosie's face about a dozen times before she nuzzles her nose under the hen's wing. Rosie and Maggie may both have had tragic pasts, but together, their future looks very bright.

There are more chickens in the world than any other bird species.

PIG AND GOAT LOVE TO SNUGGLE

LOCATION: NAPLES, FLORIDA, U.S.A.

Who says a big pig doesn't get a little lonely? When Jackie and Paul Barbush's pig, Honey, started getting larger, they knew it was time for her to move outside. But they worried about her being on her own. They wanted to find her a friend, so they decided to get a Nigerian dwarf/mini Nubian mix goat who they named Hershey. The first few days together were a little rough, with Honey recently moving from the house and Hershey being the new kid on the block. But before long, the two were great friends. In fact, in anticipation of Hershey's arrival, Paul had built them a nice big home with a comfy dog bed and soft blankets. But instead of sleeping in their spacious new digs, Honey and Hershey chose to wedge themselves into a dog crate—together! The door of the crate has been taken off, so Hershey climbs in first and scoots all the way to the back. Then Honey crawls in, and the two sleep like that: totally smooshed, but totally happy.

WHAT'S MINE IS YOURS!

PEANUT

RANJ

The average size of a rat's litter is 12 pups.

RAT FOLLOWS CAT

LOCATION: CEDARBURG, WISCONSIN, U.S.A.

Maggie Szpot wasn't sure how Ranj, her rescue cat, would react when she brought home two new pet rats. After all, most people think of cats and rats as natural enemies! But Maggie didn't need to worry. Her sweet cat was the picture of patience and gentleness, and right away one of the rats, Peanut, became smitten with the kitten. Peanut followed Ranj everywhere. He couldn't get enough of him! The enchanted rodent was constantly stroking, snuggling, and licking the cat—and Ranj allowed it. In fact, every once in a while, Ranj would return the sweet gesture and lick the top of Peanut's head. They would chase each other, rest together, and they even would eat out of Ranj's food bowl together. These friends, said Maggie, shared a sibling-like bond. Maggie began to film the pair's adorable antics, and soon the videos went viral! Sadly, Peanut has since passed away, but their friendship will live on forever in the hearts of their fans.

POTBELLIED PIG AND PUP: PALS FOR LIFE

LOCATION: BARRY, TEXAS, U.S.A.

Tuna, a Vietnamese potbellied pig, and Jack, a beagle mix, were dropped off together at the Humane Society of Texas. And while workers at the Humane Society had certainly seen animal friends before, they were surprised at how bonded this little piggy was to her pup. It soon became very clear that these two would need to be adopted together. It can be hard for one animal in need of a forever home to get adopted, and much tougher for two. Luckily, the precious pair started getting a lot of attention in the news and online. A woman named Debbie Bryan saw the duo and was happy to help. She adopted Tuna and Jack, and the two remain the best of friends. Now they have lots of space to run around, play in the yard, take naps next to each other, and splash around in their kiddie pools. Tuna still likes giving her pooch pal lots of kisses, and the future looks bright for these besties.

SEEING EYE HORSE

LOCATION: WEST GROVE, PENNSYLVANIA, U.S.A.

Lots of people have heard of guide dogs, but what about a guide ... horse? When Ashley DiFelice rescued Tonka, a 30-year-old Percheron draft horse, he became best friends with another horse named Levi. The third horse at the farm, Beau, was a bit of a third wheel. But then, sadly, Levi passed away unexpectedly, and Tonka was very, very sad. That's when Beau stepped in and helped Tonka to heal, just by being his friend. And that's not all: "As Tonka has gotten older, he has lost his sight," says Ashley. "Beau has taken on the role of his Seeing Eye dog, and he did it all on his own." These two best buddies eat together, nap together, and take walks to the water trough together. They're never far from each other, and that's the way they like it. Ashley says, "When we take one of them out of the field to see the vet or the farrier, the other will wait at the gate for his buddy to return." This is a match made in horsey heaven.

LOCATION: NEW YORK, NEW YORK, U.S.A.

When Cadbury was a young cat, he was very active—he even loved playing fetch! But as he got older, he became much less lively. Cadbury's owner, Denise DiForio, started to worry that he might need a friend to keep him company (and hopefully help get him moving). That's when Denise met Ziggy, a Chihuahua mix, during a chance encounter in New York City. She thought it must be meant to be! But when Cadbury and Ziggy first met, while they weren't aggressive or mean to each other, it wasn't exactly love at first sight, either. They just sort of stared at each other. Maybe they weren't destined to become besties. But then Ziggy had to have surgery, and he wasn't feeling well afterward. And what do you know, sweet Cadbury went right over to him and snuggled against him to comfort him. After that, the two slept snuggled together every night. Ziggy even became very protective of Cadbury. For instance, once when the aging cat slipped off the couch, Ziggy ran over to him to make sure he was okay. Cadbury, for his part, would take care of Ziggy, too, by licking him to "clean" him.

PUPPY BECOMES CAT'S PROTECTOR

COW AND GOAT FORM UNBREAKABLE BOND

LOCATION: WEST GROVE, PENNSYLVANIA, U.S.A.

Brittany Lynn, a cow, and Chip, a goat, bonded over heartbreak. While it might not seem like they would have much in common, there was one thing that united them—they both loved Elvis, a cow at Twist of Fate Farm and Sanctuary. Sadly, Elvis passed away, and when that happened, it was very hard on Brittany Lynn and Chip. As a result, the two became very close. Now they eat together, sleep next to each other, play together, and groom each other. They never leave each other's sides. "While their sizes are quite different, to them they're the same," says Ashley DiFelice, owner of the farm. "I have never seen Brittany Lynn be so gentle as when she is playing with Chip." Elvis would likely be glad to see his two buddies taking care of each other.

HAPPY HEDGEHOGS

LOCATION: WIESBADEN, HESSE, GERMANY

When Talitha Girnus adopted a hedgehog named Mr. Pokee, her dad was so smitten with the spiny sweetie that he got one of his own and named her Suna. When Mr. Pokee and Suna met each other they got right down to snuggling—and then Mr. Pokee did something that surprised everyone. "Mr. Pokee was making a really funny sound," said Talitha. "I had never heard it before; it was a bit like he was calling for Suna." The sound is sort of like a high-pitched squeak, like a dolphin might make! Since the two have become friends, the calm and collected Mr. Pokee seems to have rubbed off on Suna, who now has an easier time meeting new people. As for Mr. Pokee, who is a social media darling, his three favorite things in life are having his belly rubbed, going on adventures with Talitha, and hanging out with his snuggle buddy, Suna.

Hedgehogs are covered in prickly spines, except on their face, legs, and belly.

When hedgehogs feel nervous or threatened, they curl up into a ball, making it hard to see their face, legs, and belly.

SUNA

MR. POKEE

A baby hedgehog is called a kit, pup, or piglet.

TINY PUP BEFRIENDS BABY GOATS

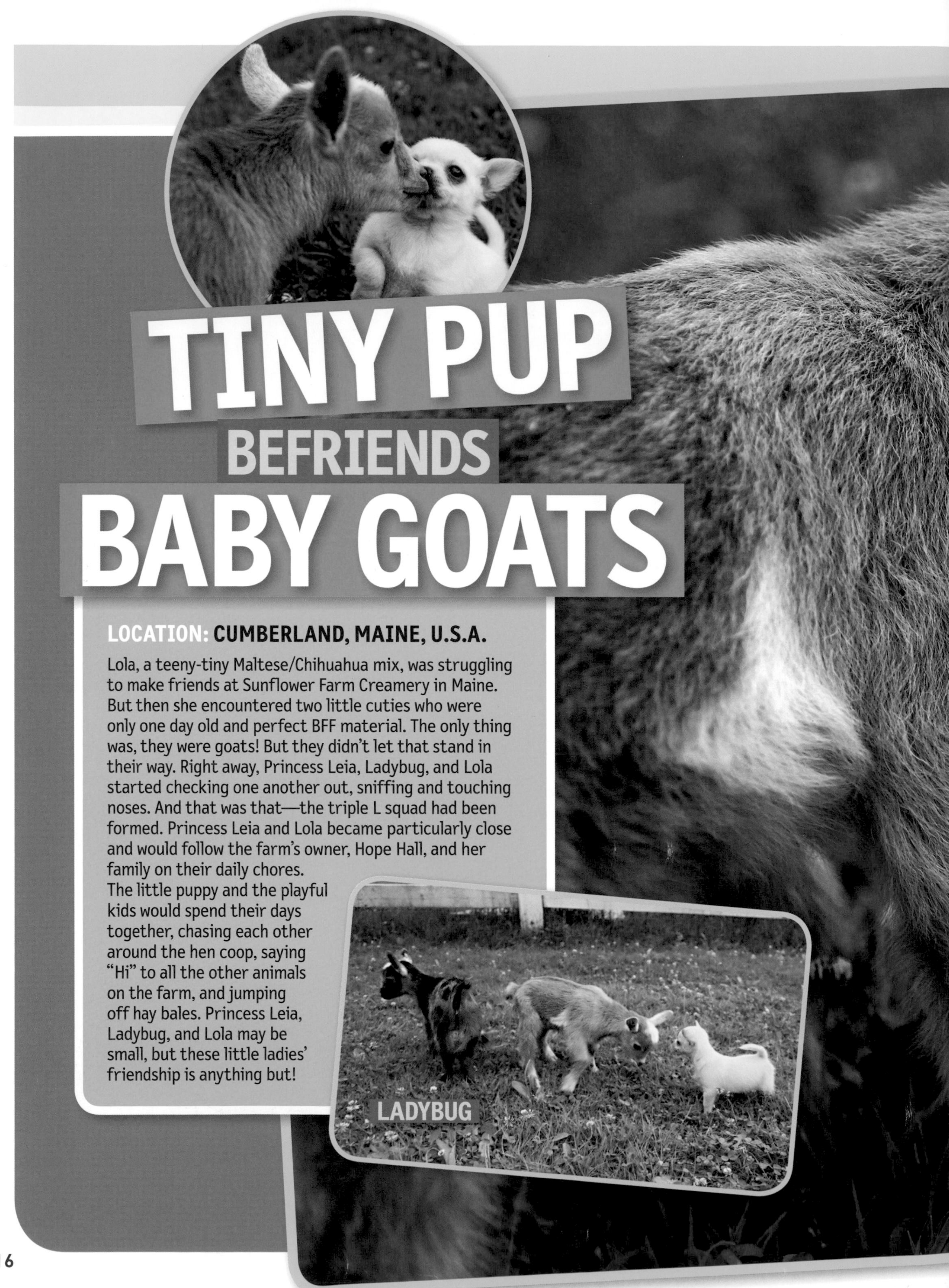

LOCATION: CUMBERLAND, MAINE, U.S.A.

Lola, a teeny-tiny Maltese/Chihuahua mix, was struggling to make friends at Sunflower Farm Creamery in Maine. But then she encountered two little cuties who were only one day old and perfect BFF material. The only thing was, they were goats! But they didn't let that stand in their way. Right away, Princess Leia, Ladybug, and Lola started checking one another out, sniffing and touching noses. And that was that—the triple L squad had been formed. Princess Leia and Lola became particularly close and would follow the farm's owner, Hope Hall, and her family on their daily chores.

The little puppy and the playful kids would spend their days together, chasing each other around the hen coop, saying "Hi" to all the other animals on the farm, and jumping off hay bales. Princess Leia, Ladybug, and Lola may be small, but these little ladies' friendship is anything but!

PRINCESS LEIA
LOLA

DOG FINDS WILD FOX FRIEND

LOCATION: NEAR OSLO, NORWAY

On one magical day in Norway, an ordinary walk in the woods turned into much more: the start of a very special friendship between a fox and a hound. Photographer Torgeir Berge was walking his dog, Tinni, when out popped a wild baby fox. The little fox wasn't scared and he wasn't aggressive—he just seemed to want a friend. The fox and Tinni immediately hit it off and spent the day romping around in the woods together, chasing and pouncing on each other, and stopping to rest side by side in the grass. For a short time the little fox, who they named Sniffer, took up residence under Torgeir's woodshed. But even when he went back to living in the woods, he would come out to see Tinni every day on his walk. Together, Tinni and Sniffer swam in ponds, climbed on fallen trees, walked on frozen lakes, frolicked, jumped, ran, and played. Their story was so special it was made into a book called *Sniffer & Tinni* by Berit Helberg—a fairy tale come true!

POTBELLIED PIG KISSES TORTOISES

LOCATION: SAN DIEGO, CALIFORNIA, U.S.A.

Illyana is a potbellied pig who likes to pal around with three tortoises named Koopa, Peach, and Gizmo. When Kathleen Gomez and her daughter Perla first introduced Illyana to the three tortoises, they weren't quite sure what to make of each other. Illyana had never met a tortoise before, and every time she went over to say "Hi," they quickly retreated into their shells. But now, they've gotten much more comfortable with one another and even let Illyana give them the occasional snout kiss. In fact, Illyana will now stick her head into Koopa's house to see what he's up to ... and, of course, check to see if he has any extra treats! It seems this funny foursome has bonded over their one shared love—grass! They love grazing in the backyard, sunning themselves, having pool parties, and foraging for food dropped by their humans. These happy pals are living proof that even the most different buds can bond over common interests!

TINY OWL HAS BIG LOVE FOR DOG

LOCATION: REMSCHEID, GERMANY

Poldi, a little owl, weighs less than a cup of sugar. But that doesn't stop this heroic hooter from trying to protect his best friend, a Belgian Malinois named Ingo. Tanja Brandt, Poldi and Ingo's owner, introduced the two unlikely buds when she adopted Poldi and brought him to live in an aviary near her home in Remscheid, Germany. Since then, they've been great friends. Once when the three were out for a walk in the woods, another owl screeched at Ingo, so Poldi swooped right in to defend his friend. He landed on Ingo's head and screeched back at the owl as if to let it know just whose dog this was! Poldi and Ingo like going for walks together and snuggling in the grass. And anytime Poldi wants a little TLC from her dog bud, she will nip at Ingo's ears to let him know. What a lucky dog—a best friend who's also a bodyguard!

DOG CALMS CHEETAH

BEST FRIENDS FUR-EVER!

CULLEN

EMMETT

Cheetahs are the fastest land mammal. They can go from 0 to 60 miles an hour (97 km/h) in just three seconds.

LOCATION:
CUMBERLAND, OHIO, U.S.A.

Emmett is a cheetah cub born at The Wilds conservation center in Cumberland, Ohio. For the first few weeks of his life he had to be raised and fed by humans. In fact, he was handled a lot by people because he had pneumonia and required around-the-clock care. Once he was better, he made the move to the Columbus Zoo and Aquarium. Cheetahs are naturally cautious animals and, on top of that, Emmett had a rough start, so the keepers at the zoo thought it was extra important that he find a friend who would help calm him and soothe him. It's important for animals' development and peace of mind that they have a friend—an animal to play with, interact with, and even cuddle with! That's where Cullen comes in—this bouncing bundle of fur was destined to become Emmett's adorable puppy pal. The two love to play together and snuggle, and because they were put together young, they will grow up with the sense that they are family. Emmett and Cullen are helping the zoo raise awareness about cheetahs to help protect the future of this endangered species.

DUCK, DUCK, GOOSE

LOCATION: ST. LOUIS, MISSOURI, U.S.A.

On Christmas Eve, Page Pardo got a call from a friend who was worried about a goose in her neighborhood. The goose's mate had been hit by a car days earlier, and ever since then she'd been wandering around, honking sadly. Page rescued the grieving goose and named her Carol (like a Christmas carol). Page put her in the passenger seat of her car, but there was only one place Carol wanted to be—Page's lap. The sweet, gentle bird wouldn't leave Page's side for weeks. But Page knew that even though she and the affectionate bird were great friends, Carol needed an animal companion. "I tried to find a male goose to buy her, to give her a new mate, but had no luck," she says. Before long, though, Page could tell that Carol was very interested in the Indian runner ducks on the farm. She would slowly approach them, but they would get super scared and run away. But Carol was determined. Every day, she would get into the pond (the ducks' favorite spot), and eventually they started letting her get closer to them. Now they are all best friends and the ducks treat her like she is one of them. Page says, "The ducks got over their fears to take Carol in as one of their flock."

GOAT REUNITES WITH DONKEY

LOCATION: GRASS VALLEY, CALIFORNIA, U.S.A.

Mr. G, a goat, and Jellybean, a donkey, were rescued together from a very bad living situation. The two had lived there together for 10 years, but no animal sanctuary could take them both in. So Mr. G was sent to Animal Place sanctuary, and there he became very depressed. He stopped eating and laid down in his stall and didn't move, barely lifting his head for days. The staff would come in to try every treat they could think of to get him to eat—molasses, sweet grain, apples—but nothing worked. Doctors examined him and said there was nothing physically wrong with Mr. G. It became clear he was grieving the loss of his friend. They needed to reunite the friends to save Mr. G! After one week apart, Jellybean joined him at the sanctuary, and the moment Mr. G smelled him, he was beside himself with happiness to be back with his best friend. Then, much to everyone's delight, within 20 minutes of being together, Mr. G began eating from Jellybean's bowl! Now the two sweet companions will stay together at a sanctuary in Grass Valley, California.

A FRIEND IN NEED

These inspiring stories are a great reminder that when you see someone struggling, sometimes the thing they need the most is a pal.

GOLA

DOG FOSTERS CHIMPS

LOCATION: LIBERIA, WEST AFRICA

Jenny and Jimmy Desmond first met Princess to foster the feisty pup. The Desmonds had been told she was unadoptable because of her wild antics. But after months of training, Princess no longer needed to look for a new home—she'd found one with the Desmonds! When Jenny and Jimmy were asked to move to Liberia, a country in West Africa, to rescue and rehabilitate orphaned chimpanzees that are victims of the illegal wildlife trade, Princess went, too. Princess not only loves spending time with the chimps, she helps them. She plays with them (they'll wrestle and play tag), protects them, and provides them with incredible comfort. One particular chimp, Portea, was in very bad shape when she got to the Desmonds. She was skinny and depressed, having suffered both physically and emotionally. While both Jenny and Jimmy gave Portea around-the-clock care, Princess helped her the most. Princess encouraged Portea to come out of her shell, and the two would play together for hours. "Portea transformed from shy and sad to happy and energetic," says Jenny. Even now that Portea lives with other chimps, when Princess goes to visit them, the now cheerful chimp is ready to play!

GLORIA

PRINCESS

JACK

DUCK CHEERS UP DOG

LOCATION: CORRYTON, TENNESSEE, U.S.A.

When Jacquie Litton's dog George lost his best dog friend, Blackie, he became very anxious and depressed. The Litton family was concerned about his health. The Littons tried and tried to help him, but it seemed that nothing would lift his spirits. Then one morning, Jacquie's husband woke up early to find a white duck asleep next to George. "We have no idea where he came from," says Jacquie. "We don't live close to any ponds that would have ducks on them. It's the strangest thing." But no matter where he came from, from the moment he arrived, it was pretty clear where the duck was going: anywhere that George went. And amazingly, Donald has helped ease George's anxiety and has brought him so much happiness. Now when the two go on walks together, George will stop and look back, waiting for Donald to catch up. They have become the best of friends. They love to snuggle together, with Donald occasionally resting his bill on George. "George has finally found some peace," says Jacquie. "We think Blackie sent Donald to George to help mend his broken heart."

DOG BECOMES CAT'S BODYGUARD

LOCATION: LAKE MARY, FLORIDA, U.S.A.

An animal control officer found Idgie and Ruth sitting at the end of a stranger's driveway in rural Florida. Idgie the dachshund was covered in ants. But even that couldn't keep her from her mission: protecting her best friend, a disabled cat named Ruth. When the officer finally got past Ruth's barking bodyguard, he saw right away that she didn't have full use of her legs and wasn't able to stand. At first, the officer separated Idgie and Ruth, since dogs and cats are usually kept apart at the animal control facility. But it wasn't long before Idgie made it very clear that the arrangement wasn't going to work. Idgie cried and howled until the workers realized that these two were much happier when they were together and reunited the devoted pair. Idgie and Ruth were rescued by the owner of Hollywood Houndz Boutique, Spa & Hotel, and lived a life of luxury and fantastic friendship.

DOG ADOPTS GOAT

LOCATION: DEVON, ENGLAND, U.K.

One of the coolest things about animals is how they step in to help others who need a mom or a dad. And not only will they help babies from different families, they'll act as a parent figure for an animal from an entirely different species. That's exactly what happened when Billy the boxer met a baby goat named Lilly. Elizabeth Tozer, owner of Pennywell Farm in Devon, England, rescued Lilly after she had been abandoned by her mother. Because Lilly was the smallest in the litter, her mom stopped caring for her to focus on the two stronger, healthier babies. Elizabeth began bottle-feeding Lilly and caring for her. One day, while Elizabeth was cleaning Lilly after a feeding, Billy noticed what was going on and his daddy instincts kicked in. He took over cleaning Lilly, licking her, and nuzzling her. From that point on, the two were a daddy-daughter duo and never left each other's sides. Now they play together, meander around the farm together, and even curl up together when it's time for bed.

KOALA HAS PLUSH PAL

LOCATION: QUEENSLAND, AUSTRALIA

Sometimes a friend can come from the place you least expect. That was certainly true for a scared little koala named Shayne who was rescued by the Australia Zoo Wildlife Hospital. Shayne was found up in a tree, where he'd been chased by crows after his mother passed away. He needed to get checked out by the doctors to make sure he hadn't been injured during the ordeal. But little Shayne was very scared. So the doctor decided to give him a friend that could comfort him and calm him. The little friend the doctor gave him was a plush koala toy, and it worked! Little Shayne clung to the cute stuffed animal. Shayne is already feeling happier and calmer, and he's been eating and gaining weight. Shayne will now be taken care of and taught important life skills by a caregiver at the wildlife hospital before he is released back into the wild. Even stuffed friends are important!

PIT BULL BONDS WITH BABY BUNNY

LOCATION: NAPLES, FLORIDA, U.S.A.

Rando the pit bull showed up one day in Jackie and Paul Barbush's yard. He was a stray dog with no collar, he was hungry, and he seemed desperate for a family. Jackie and Paul decided that they wanted him to be a permanent part of *their* family, so they invited him into the house. "He was so sweet," says Jackie. "He seemed really grateful to be inside." Jackie and Paul, who are huge animal lovers, often bring in animals in need, as well as foster kittens from time to time. Right away it was clear that Rando loved the baby kittens. He was so gentle and sweet with them and seemed to really understand that he needed to be careful. So when one of Jackie's students gave her a baby bunny, she wasn't too concerned about how she'd get along with Rando. But she couldn't have known just how well they'd hit it off! The little bunny, named Harvey, likes to bite Rando's toenails and lick his face. And as for Rando? Well, he happily lets her. The two like to jump around together and snuggle lots. Rando even lets his bunny bud eat out of his food bowl. For Rando, this is truly a rags-to-riches tale.

DOG PROTECTS OWL

LOCATION: HAMPSHIRE, ENGLAND, U.K.

These two friends took a while to get to know each other, but their friendship was worth the wait! When a greyhound named Torque was just six months old, he was introduced to a three-day-old long-eared owl called Shrek. Shrek was being cared for by the head falconer, John Picton, at the Liberty's Owl, Raptor and Reptile Centre in England. John, who owned Torque as a pet, introduced the two unlikely pals slowly, first letting Shrek eat his meals in the same room as Torque. Then he began to hold Shrek and allow the curious Torque to sniff him to get comfortable with the fluffy fellow. Now the two have become good friends. Torque even protects his feathered friend by putting the cute little owl between his legs to make sure he's safe. They love to play together, explore John's house, lounge in the grass, and even watch the occasional TV show—what feathery, furry fun!

DOGS LOVE THEIR BUNNY

LOCATION: PERTH, AUSTRALIA

Abby Flynn's dogs were quite comfortable with their situation. There was Albi, a 4-year-old border collie/kelpie mix and Max, a 15-year-old cocker spaniel. Over time, the two had become like brothers, always snuggling and checking in on each other. So when Abby's husband gave her a mini lop rabbit named Arlo for her birthday, she was a little nervous about how the pups would react. Not only would Arlo be the new kid in town, but she was so tiny. But Abby needn't have worried. It was clear from the get-go that Albi and Max meant Arlo no harm. "Max was really gentle with her straightaway," says Abby. "Arlo would climb all over him and he was never bothered by it." In fact, Max often shares his dog bed with the beautiful bunny. And as for Albi? He's smitten! He's so affectionate, in fact, that sometimes Abby and her husband will find a soaking wet Arlo, because Albi has been licking her. He follows her everywhere she goes and has even learned how to open the hutch where she sleeps at night so he can play with her. And as for Arlo? Being around such big dogs has made her one brave bunny. Says Abby, "She isn't scared of anything!"

ALPACAS MAKE PERFECT PAIR

LOCATION: VAUXHALL, ALBERTA, CANADA

Jack and Jill, both alpacas, were born just weeks apart at Leslie Unruh's alpaca farm. From the moment these brave babies met each other, they've been inseparable. Leslie kept trying to put Jill back with her mom, but Jill would get so sad anytime she was away from Jack. Both Jack and Jill seemed to be their happiest when they were together. To this day they still like to eat, sleep, and hang out side by side. These two might behave like twins, but they don't look too much alike. "Jack is a large cria (or baby alpaca), one of the biggest we've had," says Leslie, "and Jill is the tiniest one we've ever had." But don't tell them that—they don't seem to have noticed they're not brother and sister.

DOLPHIN IS BEST FRIENDS WITH SEA LION

MIRI

LOCATION: COFFS HARBOUR, AUSTRALIA

If you ever visit the clear waters of the Dolphin Marine Magic zoological park in Australia, you'll find a beautiful friendship between a bottlenose dolphin and a sea lion. Miri the sea lion and Jet the dolphin met one day during a free playtime, when the sea lions and the dolphins get together to socialize. Since then, these two sweet swimmers have made their friendship BFF-official. They chase each other around Jet's pool, share snacks (though sometimes Miri will take them right out of Jet's mouth), and even chat a little (Jet makes clicking noises and Miri barks back). Miri is so smitten with her bottlenose buddy that she's been known to stop what she's doing just to give Jet a kiss. These two sure are making a splash!

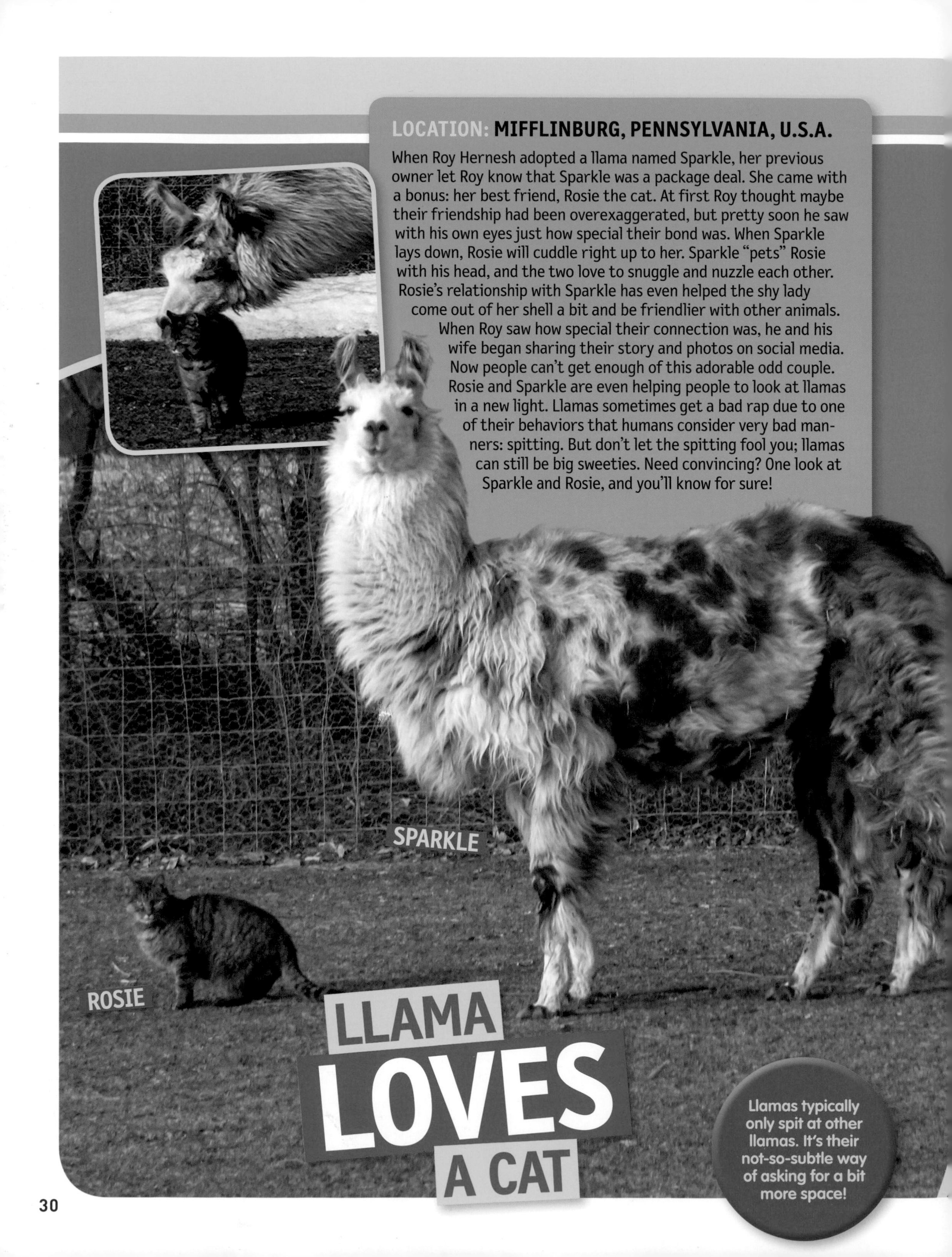

LLAMA LOVES A CAT

LOCATION: MIFFLINBURG, PENNSYLVANIA, U.S.A.

When Roy Hernesh adopted a llama named Sparkle, her previous owner let Roy know that Sparkle was a package deal. She came with a bonus: her best friend, Rosie the cat. At first Roy thought maybe their friendship had been overexaggerated, but pretty soon he saw with his own eyes just how special their bond was. When Sparkle lays down, Rosie will cuddle right up to her. Sparkle "pets" Rosie with his head, and the two love to snuggle and nuzzle each other. Rosie's relationship with Sparkle has even helped the shy lady come out of her shell a bit and be friendlier with other animals. When Roy saw how special their connection was, he and his wife began sharing their story and photos on social media. Now people can't get enough of this adorable odd couple. Rosie and Sparkle are even helping people to look at llamas in a new light. Llamas sometimes get a bad rap due to one of their behaviors that humans consider very bad manners: spitting. But don't let the spitting fool you; llamas can still be big sweeties. Need convincing? One look at Sparkle and Rosie, and you'll know for sure!

Llamas typically only spit at other llamas. It's their not-so-subtle way of asking for a bit more space!

FOX FINDS FRIEND

LOCATION: LOCUST GROVE, GEORGIA, U.S.A.

Foxes and dogs might look similar, but they usually avoid each other. However, Dublin the German shepherd and Oscar the one-eyed silver fox were put together at Noah's Ark Animal Sanctuary in Georgia when Oscar was just one month old. Oscar needed a friend to play with, but also an animal who could be comforting and nurturing to him, since he was just a baby. Dublin could do that and more! Dublin acted like the best babysitter ever, taking care of Oscar and playing games. One of their favorite games is a version of hide-and-seek: Oscar likes to bury his favorite toys, and Dublin then goes and digs them up! They can do this again and again until one or both of them gets tired. Now that Oscar is older, he lives with other foxes in the sanctuary. But at least once a week, he still visits Dublin for games and snuggles.

SHEEP ACTS LIKE A DOG

PET

DICE

LOCATION: ULLAPOOL, SCOTLAND, U.K.

When Pet the sheep was a baby, she was sick, weak, and struggling to stay warm during the winter in Scotland. So her owner, Mairi Mackenzie, brought her inside the house. It was there that she met one of the family's dogs, a border collie named Dice. Dice realized right away that Pet needed some extra TLC, and the sweet dog was more than happy to give it to her. Dice snuggled Pet and doted on her, and soon enough the other dogs also accepted Pet into the pack. Then, as Pet grew, it became clear she thought of herself more as a dog than as a sheep! She loves to play with the dogs, and even though she's not nearly as fast or agile, she does her best to keep up. She runs with the dogs, jumping this way and that, lifting all four legs in the air at once. Pet goes on daily walks with the dogs, and she even tries to wag her tail like them. It's hard to get much cuter than that!

PENGUIN TRAVELS TO FIND FRIEND

LOCATION: SCHNECKSVILLE, PENNSYLVANIA, U.S.A.

Finding a friend isn't always easy, but when you find a great one, it's definitely worth the wait. Penguin Don and her sister Dewey both lived at Saginaw Michigan's Children's Zoo. They were best friends and very happy, but when Dewey found a mate, she stopped hanging out with Don. The other penguins at the zoo didn't really seem to want to be friends with Don, either. The African Penguin Species Survival Plan Program (SSP) decided that it would be best for Don to move to another zoo where she might be more welcome and—hey!—maybe she'd even find a mate. Well, that's exactly what happened! Don moved to the Lehigh Valley Zoo in Pennsylvania and has been accepted into the colony. She also has a male companion: a little fella named Clytee. Clytee brings Don pebbles, twigs, and other materials that would help her to make a nest. The two lovebirds also groom each other, and the veterinarians at the zoo are hopeful they may even produce some penguin chicks!

DOG AND PRAIRIE DOG PLAYMATES

LOCATION: FORT WORTH, TEXAS, U.S.A.

When a German shepherd named Banksy first met Prince, a prairie dog, Prince weighed only six ounces (170 g; about the same size as a large orange). Banksy was baffled by how to play with his pocket-size pal. Prince, however, was up to the challenge! Before long, this sweet little odd couple had figured out how to have fun together. Banksy is very careful with Prince; sometimes he'll open his mouth and gently move his head around as little Prince grabs and nibbles at his snout. Prince has also started to take an interest in Banksy's toys, though his favorite way to play with them is to wait until Banksy has one in his mouth and then chase him around the house. Now that they've gotten more comfortable with each other, Prince will give Banksy a "prairie dog kiss," which is how prairie dogs greet each other in the wild. Other times, Prince will curl up by Banksy's belly on the couch. "Prince actually gets more excited to run out of his cage and greet Banksy than he does to see me most of the time," says his owner, Taylor Williams. "They are a dynamic duo, and they make everyone smile who witnesses their brotherly love!"

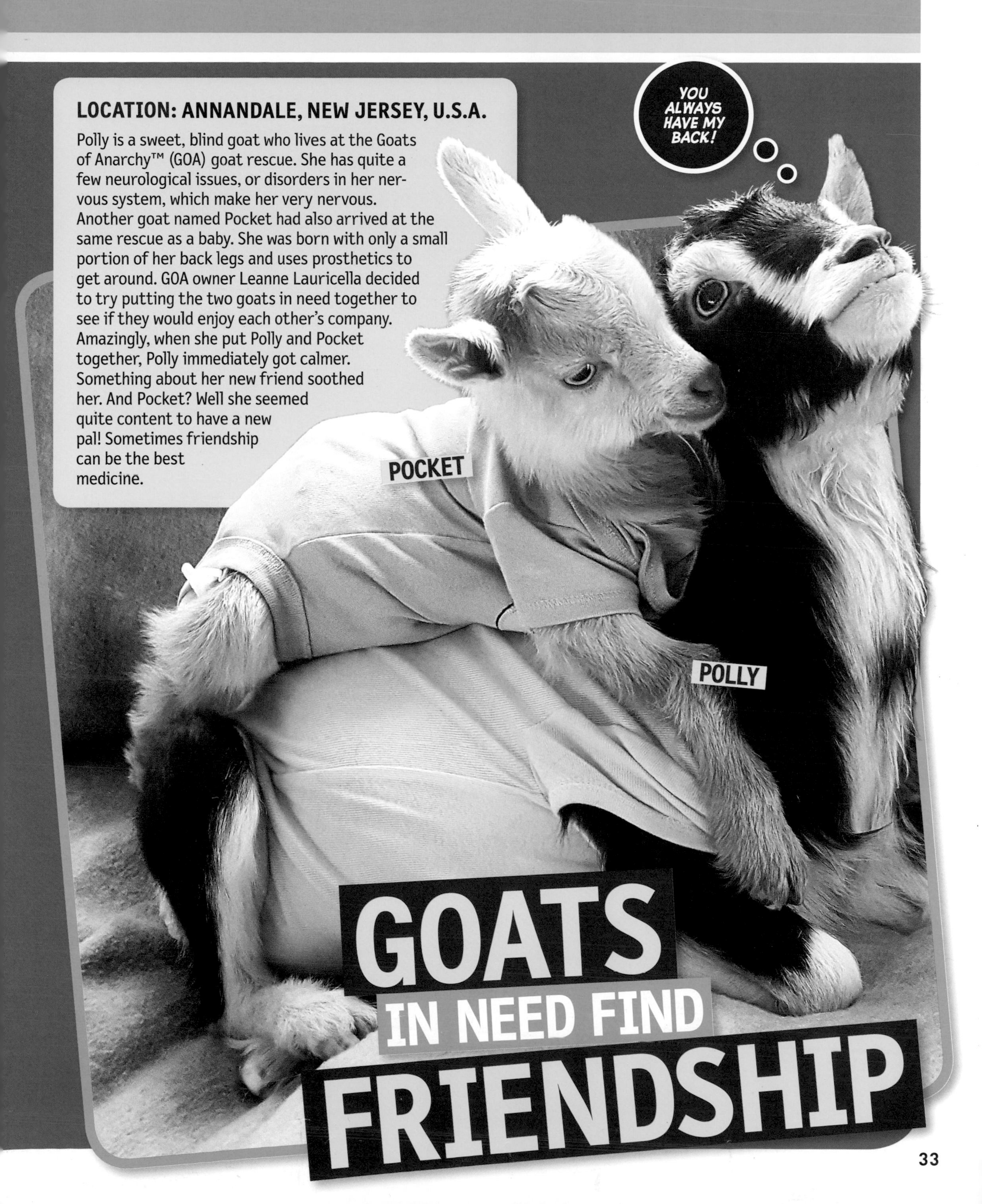

LOCATION: ANNANDALE, NEW JERSEY, U.S.A.

Polly is a sweet, blind goat who lives at the Goats of Anarchy™ (GOA) goat rescue. She has quite a few neurological issues, or disorders in her nervous system, which make her very nervous. Another goat named Pocket had also arrived at the same rescue as a baby. She was born with only a small portion of her back legs and uses prosthetics to get around. GOA owner Leanne Lauricella decided to try putting the two goats in need together to see if they would enjoy each other's company. Amazingly, when she put Polly and Pocket together, Polly immediately got calmer. Something about her new friend soothed her. And Pocket? Well she seemed quite content to have a new pal! Sometimes friendship can be the best medicine.

GOATS IN NEED FIND FRIENDSHIP

FARMYARD FRIENDS

LOCATION: BLAIRSTOWN, NEW JERSEY, U.S.A.

Tamala Lester started The Barnyard Sanctuary, a nonprofit organization in New Jersey, to help people find happy homes for their pet farm animals that they could no longer care for. Today, it's home to more than 700 rescued farm animals, including cows, horses, donkeys, mules, goats, sheep, llamas, alpacas, pigs, rabbits, cats, and multiple types of birds. Read on to learn about some of the farmyard friends that call The Barnyard home!

ROO

The loose skin below a rooster's beak is called a wattle.

ROOSTER LOVES PIGGYBACK RIDES

This rooster picked the perfect pals! When Tamala rescued Roo the rooster, she couldn't put him in with the other roosters right away because she was worried they might be aggressive with him. Instead, she let him loose in the pasture and gave him the chance to decide where he wanted to live. Surprisingly, Roo settled in with the herd—with goats, sheep, llamas, alpacas, calves, baby water buffalo, pigs, hogs, and more! This calm, friendly bird loves all of the animals and they love him. One of Roo's favorite things to do with his barnyard buds is to stand on their backs. Sometimes he'll lie down and other times, he'll stay perched up there as they walk around (or at least he does for as long as he can hold on!). When it comes to his animal besties, this adventurous, quirky little rooster definitely has their backs.

PIG THINKS SHE'S A DOG

Maggie is a pig who thinks she's a dog. She was someone's pet and lived inside their house along with three pit bulls. But when the family sadly couldn't care for her any longer, they called Tamala. Tamala has tried getting her to socialize with other pigs on the farm, but Maggie isn't having it—she only wants to be with her dog buds. So she sleeps in a doghouse next to another occupied by an actual dog, Otie. "Maggie is very territorial over her doghouse," says Tamala. "We have to sneak to clean it when she is not around." There is only one person Maggie lets inside, and that's her best friend—not a dog, but a cat named Choc-o-Latte ("Latte" for short)! Sweet, super-friendly Latte loves her piggy pal so much that she crawls into her doghouse at night and sleeps, curled up, on her back.

POTBELLIED PIG PROTECTS GOAT

When someone saw a baby potbellied pig on the side of the road, they called Tamala straightaway. She ran home, grabbed a cat carrier and a pastry, and went back to rescue the pig. Tamala named the pig Cherry after the type of tasty Danish that lured him into the carrier. Because Tamala hadn't planned to take in a new pig that day, she didn't have an open spot for Cherry on the farm. So she put him in with a sick goat named Delilah. Delilah had a disease that affects sheep and goats, so she had to be kept separate from other animals that might catch it. Cherry, realizing that Delilah was sick, became her protector. Whenever a doctor or someone came into the pen to examine Delilah, Cherry stood in front of her and checked them out to make sure they meant no harm. Delilah also suffered from arthritis, and if she had been lying down too long (which isn't good for her), Cherry would nudge her with his nose to get her to stand up and walk around. Cherry is a friend as sweet as his name!

One reason pigs roll in the mud is to protect their sensitive skin from the sun.

DELILAH

CHERRY

DOG AND HEDGEHOG CELEBRITIES

LOCATION: SURREY, ENGLAND, U.K.

When Maya, a sweet miniature dachshund, first met a roly-poly hedgehog called Minnie, Maya had no idea what the strange animal in front of her was. Maya was used to her dachshund friend, Peanut. But this animal had spikes and was even smaller than she was! Since she'd never met a hedgehog before, Maya got a little too close a little too fast, and Minnie put her spikes up and curled into a ball. From then on, Maya learned not to approach the mini Minnie too quickly, and the two became fast friends. The petite pals quickly took the Internet by storm and gained tons of fans on social media! Minnie loved having her back petted, eating chicken, digging for bugs in the garden, and snuggling with Maya and Peanut. Together, the tiny trio spent their days delighting their owner, Natasha Fernandes, and living the celebrity lifestyle.

KITTENS WELCOME DUCK

LOCATION: OGILVIE, MINNESOTA, U.S.A.

When Katie Stulc and Nick DuFoe adopted Penny, a Muscovy duck, their only concern was introducing her to their two new kittens, Leonard and Sheldon. After all, cats and birds don't have the most spotless track record together. But sometimes friendships blossom from unexpected places. When they first met Penny, the cats weren't the slightest bit cliquey or aggressive. They immediately welcomed Penny into their pack, and the three have become best friends. The cats go out to her pen in the morning and then the three head to the front yard, where they spend their days together, walking and waddling around, lying in the sun, and just hanging out and being buds. Every once in a while, Penny will pick at their fur with her beak (like she would to another duck) and the cats will gently bat her away with their paws. But the three are so comfortable together, from time to time the cats even wedge themselves into Penny's crate with her, creating an adorable mash of fur and feathers.

GOAT PREFERS HER SHEEP PALS

LOCATION: LOS ANGELES, CALIFORNIA, U.S.A.

When Sofie the goat was rescued and brought to Farm Sanctuary in Los Angeles, she wasn't really interested in hanging out with the other goats. While they were out roughhousing and running around in the pasture, she was much calmer and more reserved. In fact, she seemed much more at home with the sheep! In particular, she seemed to get along quite well with a sheep named Bela. Bela is a strong-willed, feisty leader. He was given over to Farm Sanctuary after he was purchased by a farmer but then got into fights with the farmer's dogs. But now Bela has found a situation that suits him. At Farm Sanctuary, he leads a herd of sheep with Sofie, his goat companion, by his side. The two are inseparable and have a very unique, unbreakable bond. They like to nuzzle each other, take naps together, and take walks together around the farm. Not baaad!

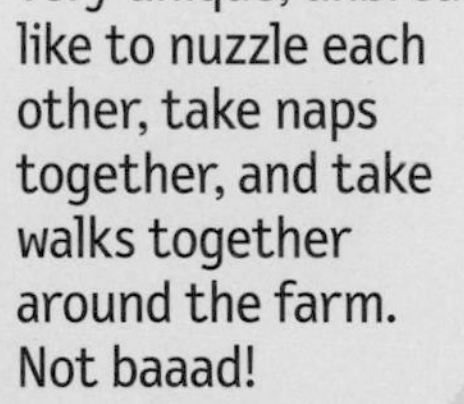

DOGS ADOPT COW

LOCATION: MIDWAY, ARKANSAS, U.S.A.

When Moonpie the mini cow was rescued and brought to an animal refuge, she was still young enough that she needed to be bottle-fed and kept indoors. That's where Moonpie met two rescued bull terriers, Spackle and Cadbury. Right away, Spackle treated Moonpie—who was already bigger than the 35-pound (16-kg) pup—like she was her puppy. Spackle loves baby animals and wouldn't leave mini Moonpie's side. And Cadbury, just a baby himself, was smitten with the calf, too. The dogs played with her, snuggled her, and licked her face after she ate. Moonpie has since moved outside, but her pen is right next to the dogs', and Spackle and Cadbury pop over frequently to visit with their bovine buddy. These three are as sweet as candy!

LYNX HAS HOUSE CAT COMPANION

LOCATION: ST. PETERSBURG, RUSSIA

Everyone has that friend who's just a little bit wilder than them ... and that's definitely the case for these two kitty companions, Linda and Dusja. Linda is a type of wild cat called a lynx, and Dusja is an ordinary house cat. But these two don't let their differences get in the way. When Linda was just six weeks old, the zookeepers at the Leningrad Zoo in St. Petersburg, Russia, thought she might like a companion. They brought in Dusja, who was just a kitten as well. Now, years later, they're two peas in a pod. They live together in Linda's enclosure (much to the delight of zoo visitors) and they play together, cuddle, and clean each other. These two are the cat's meow!

LOCATION: CAMERON PARK, CALIFORNIA, U.S.A.

Did somebunny say adventure? Freckles, Fuzzy, and Finnegan are three adorable Holland lop bunnies who love exploring together. They adore hopping around the yard, munching on grass, eating bananas, and snuggling up together once their adventuring is done. Each bunny has a very particular personality and role in the group. Freckles is very laid back and is the only one who really loves being petted. Fuzzy, the only girl in the group, dotes on the others but has a feisty streak. Then there's Finnegan, the youngest and smallest of the crew. He scares easily, so he's always on the lookout for possible dangers. Together, these three form an unstoppable team—and a very hoppy family! "They have a deep connection and understanding," says their owner, Tessa Reber. "They have formed a truly unconditional family bond." Sometimes, the best friends you'll make are your very own family.

ONE HOPPY FAMILY

DALLY THE HORSE-RIDING DOG

LOCATION:
NEAR SPOKANE, WASHINGTON, U.S.A.

When Francesca Carsen and Steve Rother rescued a miniature horse named Spanky, he was a bit of a troublemaker, to say the least. Spanky would get into fights with humans and other horses, sometimes kicking and even biting them. But Francesca and Steve knew that with the right training Spanky could be a happy, well-behaved horse. Soon after they rescued Spanky, they adopted a tiny Jack Russell terrier puppy. They named her Dally. Spanky and Dally seemed to have a normal horse and dog relationship, with Dally watching while Francesca and Steve taught Spanky to jump and do tricks. But one day, Dally jumped from a stool right up onto Spanky's back! Amazingly, both Spanky and Dally had a blast! From there, this unlikely twosome became the best of friends. Today, they travel around the country performing tricks together for audiences. When Spanky approaches a jump, Dally leans forward with Spanky's mane between her paws. Not only are they an incredible sight to see, but their friendship has made Spanky a kinder, happier horse. Now he gets along with humans and horse friends alike. Spanky and Dally are proof of just how powerful a friendship can be!

DALLY
IT'S SHOW-TIME!
SPANKY

PUP BEFRIENDS GUINEA PIGS

LOCATION: SAN FRANCISCO, CALIFORNIA, U.S.A.

When Kristy Gamayo and her partner, Alicia, adopted a pit bull puppy named Moki, they decided to introduce her to the whole family right away. So when Moki arrived at her new home she also met her two guinea pig siblings, Frida and Pandora. Moki was very curious, and right away she began sniffing and licking her new furry friends. The feeling was mutual! The guinea pigs were fascinated by their new, much bigger sister. Whenever they got the chance, they would crawl up to her to smell her and sometimes nibble at Moki's nose. But the gentle pup didn't seem to mind. These three are very comfortable around one another and love snuggling most of all. Sweet Moki even brings Frida and Pandora her toys and bones. With such tiny mouths, all the "piggies" can really do to show their appreciation is sniff them. But as the saying goes, the nose knows—and these guinea pigs definitely know a friend when they sniff one.

PORCUPINE PALS WITH PUPS

MACARTHUR

MAUDE

LOCATION: LAKE TAHOE, CALIFORNIA, U.S.A.

It's not every day you see a porcupine hanging out with three bulldogs, but that's exactly what you'll find if you visit Ann Bryant's home. A wildlife rehabilitation specialist, Ann rescued a pregnant porcupine she found injured on the side of the road. Three days later, baby porcupine Maude was born in Ann's living room as her bulldogs looked on. Maude has never known life without her bulldog buddies, and together they are a tight-knit team of adventurers. They go for walks in the woods, warm themselves in the sun, and play together in the snow. Maude and the three dogs, Millicent, Mosey, and MacArthur, love to go for rides in boats, kayaks, or—Maude's favorite—a wagon! Maude's sweetness shines through to everyone she meets—porcupine quills and all. Ann is very comfortable handling Maude: She gives her baths and brushes her quills just like she does for the bulldogs' fur.

"Maude loves to be held and snuggled," says Ann. "It seems odd to most people that an animal dressed in sharp spears can actually be a cuddle-bunny. But, that she is." And she's the biggest cuddle-bunny of all for her best dog friends.

Maude's favorite foods are almonds, acorns, strawberries, Cheerios, corn on the cob, pears, and roses.

ALPACA IS CRAZY FOR CATS

LOCATION: ALBERTA, CANADA

Lacey the alpaca was born at a farm in Canada called A to Z Alpacas. Unfortunately, her mother wasn't able to feed her. So the farm's owner, Leslie Unruh, stepped in and began bottle-feeding tiny Lacey. Seeing as how she was a baby (and, of course, an animal), she wasn't always the tidiest eater. But that definitely wasn't a problem for the cats on the farm. In fact, they loved it! The milk would drip from the bottles, and all of a sudden the cats were hanging around more and more, hoping for a chance to get whatever milk Lacey left behind. Then, even when she wasn't eating, Lacey and the cats began spending their time together. The cats would sleep with her at night, snuggling up with Lacey to keep warm. They would play together, roam around the farm together, and lie together on the porch and press their noses together. What began as a means to milk blossomed into a full-blown best friendship.

LACEY

GORILLA HAS PET RABBIT

SAMANTHA

LOCATION: ERIE, PENNSYLVANIA, U.S.A.

An elderly gorilla named Samantha, who lived at a Pennsylvania zoo, was without a friend after her companion passed away. Because she was older, the zookeepers didn't think it would be wise to put her in with other gorillas, but they wanted her to have a buddy. Just like with humans, having a friend helps animals stay mentally and physically healthy. So, they carefully and slowly introduced Samantha to a Dutch rabbit named Panda. Zoo visitors loved seeing Panda happily hopping around Samantha's enclosure. Samantha, who had a very gentle, sweet personality, really loved Panda and would scratch her under her chin, pat her fur, and even share her food with her. Samantha and Panda lived out the rest of their days together, happy to have found a good friend.

Gorillas are mostly herbivores and eat stems, bamboo shoots, and fruits.

PANDA

SOMEBUNNY LOVES YOU, SAMANTHA!

PUP PICKS OUT KITTEN

LOCATION: LUBBOCK, TEXAS, U.S.A.

When Christina Cross wanted to bring a kitten into the family, she wanted the input of one very important member—her tamaskan puppy, Raven. So she brought her sweet pup along to the local animal shelter to help her pick out a new friend. The woman working at the shelter brought each kitten out one by one so that Raven could be introduced. Raven immediately hit it off with the first one; they sniffed and nuzzled each other. After that, she met three more kittens, but the shy pup either didn't show much interest in them or would nervously back away. When they brought out the first kitten again, whom they later named Woodhouse, they knew they had found the right cat for the whole family. Raven and Woodhouse are the cutest companions still to this day. Their favorite games are wrestling and tag. They even share treats (the first day they were together, Raven held his peanut butter rawhide in his paws so that Woodhouse could lick it). They're pretty paw-fect!

LLAMA COMFORTS SHEEP

YODA

FELICITY

LOCATION: LOS ANGELES, CALIFORNIA, U.S.A.

Felicity is a sheep who was rescued from a situation in which she was severely mistreated. She was found with 12 other sheep, but she was the only one of her particular breed—a Barbados blackbelly. She also was unlike the other sheep because she hadn't bonded with any of the others. Her only friend was a goat named Claire who'd been rescued from the same place. Felicity and Claire arrived at Farm Sanctuary together. But after a while, Claire started hanging out in the large goat and sheep herd, and Felicity didn't quite feel comfortable there. So she befriended a sweet, gentle llama named Yoda. Felicity and Yoda love going for walks on the hillside, grazing, and napping together. And, bonus: Felicity can fit beneath Yoda, which is a nice comfort for the anxious sheep. As Felicity gets more and more comfortable at Farm Sanctuary, she's also gotten a little less nervous around the humans. She's even progressed to taking treats from them, something she wouldn't have dared to do a few months ago. Maybe the sweet, soothing llama has more in common with a certain Jedi master than just a name.

ODD COUPLES

Sometimes what makes a good friend is a mystery mush of secret ingredients. There's no real rhyme or reason, there's just that feeling that maybe, just maybe, you were made for each other.

ELEPHANT LOVES DOTING DOG

LOCATION: HOHENWALD, TENNESSEE, U.S.A.

When elephants arrive at The Elephant Sanctuary in Tennessee, they often pair up and spend their days with one other elephant—sort of like a bestie. But when Tarra, an 8,700-pound (3,946-kg) elephant, met Bella, a stray dog who took refuge at the sanctuary, they formed their own special friendship. Tarra didn't need another elephant friend so long as she had Bella. The sweet pair became inseparable. They'd eat together, sleep together, play in the woods together, and wade in the water together. Tarra would even pet Bella's belly with her trunk. One day, Bella was injured and had to be away from Tarra while she received medical care. The entire time Bella was away, Tarra stood guard right outside the medical building, waiting to make sure her fluffy friend was okay. Seeing how much they missed each other, workers at the sanctuary began carrying Bella out for daily visits with Tarra. Bella would wag her tail with happiness and Tarra would stretch her trunk through the fence to touch her sweet puppy pal. Tarra and Bella's friendship proves that great things come in all sizes.

BIG DOG HAS PETITE PALS

LOCATION: DENVER, COLORADO, U.S.A.

Shortly after Tara Dara got a tiny little hedgehog named Mackinnon for her son's birthday, she adopted a Saint Bernard named Beethoven. The first day the two met, they immediately got nose to nose on the kitchen floor. And while they couldn't look any more different—they're pretty much complete opposites—there was no fear or aggression. In fact, these two were insta-buds. Beethoven lets Mackinnon and the family's guinea pig, Gertie, climb on him while he relaxes. Then when the little ones are ready to move, they just slide off his big body. Beethoven weighs 160 pounds (72.6 kg), Gertie weighs about three pounds (1.7 kg), and Mackinnon? She weighs just one little pound (0.5 kg). But Beethoven takes his role as big brother seriously. He corrals Gertie and Mackinnon when they're out in the yard, making sure they don't go anywhere they're not supposed to. "Gertie and Mackinnon never fret or appear threatened by Beethoven," says Tara. "They all just gravitate toward each other." Beethoven is yet another great example of how looks can be deceiving. Sometimes the sweetest souls come in surprising (and super slobbery) packages.

GOOSE GUARDS DONKEY

LOCATION: RAPIDAN, VIRGINIA, U.S.A.

When Bub's mate passed away, his owner, Lolly Busey, didn't think Bub would make it. The 44-year-old donkey was truly heartbroken. But one day a new hope for Bub came out of the clear blue sky—a goose named Goose. The two were instant friends. And while Goose can fly away at any time, he chooses to stay right by Bub's side. The sweet pair walk around their pasture together and lay side by side in the hay. Goose acts as Bub's personal bodyguard and will chase away ducks, sheep, goats, or humans—anyone that gets too close, which can be a challenge when the vet comes to visit! Together, Goose and Bub talk to the cows and goats in neighboring pastures (Bub brays and Goose honks) and eat treats. Goose even preens Bub, trying to fix Bub's "feathers." "The pair seem connected by an invisible cord," says Lolly. "They are never more than a heartbeat away from each other." Goose came into Bub's life when he needed a friend the most, and side by side they've filled their days with love and fun.

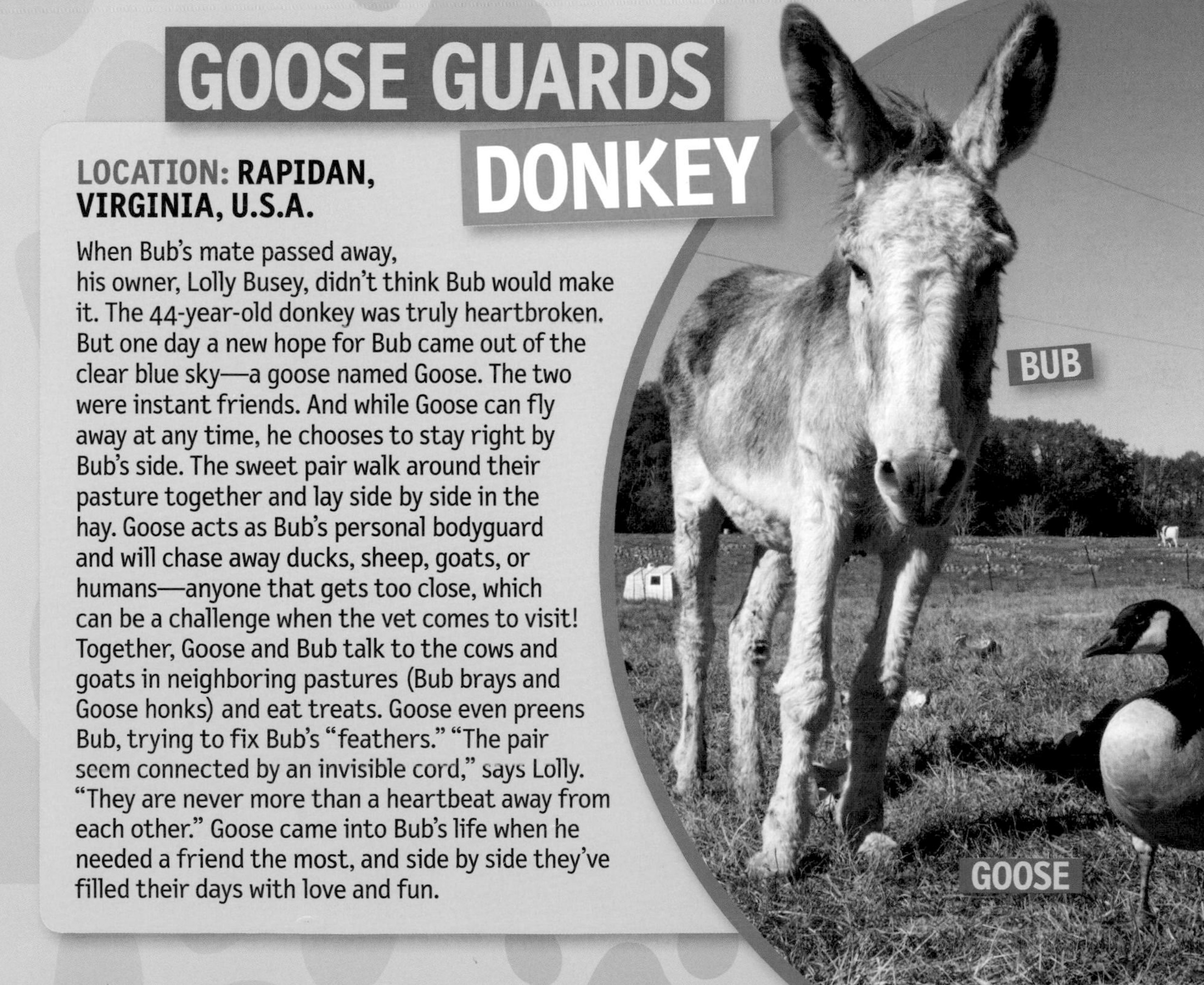

CAT CARETAKER

LOCATION: TE HORO, NEW ZEALAND

Sometimes cats can get a reputation for being standoffish or cold. Well, when it comes to this special cat at Free as a Hawk Refuge in New Zealand, that couldn't be further from the truth. The cat's name is Kitten, and she is exceptionally warm and nurturing. Kitten's owner suspects that this is because she was bottle-fed as a baby. Kitten seems determined to return the kindness she was shown as a tiny tot, and she has taken care of all sorts of animals at the sanctuary that need a mother figure, including ducks, lambs, and possums. Most recently, this fantastic feline is caring for a baby emu who hatched at the nursery. The two have become quite cozy with one another—they snuggle together on the couch and Kitten grooms the emu's long neck.

KITTEN

DOG AND PIG SNUGGLE

LOCATION: SYRACUSE, NEW YORK, U.S.A.

When Bo the bullmastiff met Peaches the potbellied pig, Bo had never seen a pig before ... and Peaches had never seen a dog! While Peaches was a little bit nervous, Bo was super curious. What was this little pink oink machine? It didn't take long before they both knew exactly what the other was—a friend! These days, the unlikely pair's favorite way to pass the time is by snuggling up together on the couch. They also love to lie in the sun and eat peanut butter out of their separate toys. (Peaches will share a lot of things, but food isn't one of them!) During playtime, their owners, Mike Derecola and Tori Trovato, shout "Go, Peaches, go!" which whips Peaches into a frenzy, causing her to zoom around the yard as Bo chases her. "It's hilarious to watch," says Tori. Bo is a goofy, gentle giant, Peaches is a queen bee, and together they are the best of friends.

SWEET PUP PLAYS WITH GOAT PAL

BAA BAA BOW BOW

DEAN

MICHAEL

LOCATION: WOODSTOWN, NEW JERSEY, U.S.A.

These best buds are practically a comedy duo! An orphaned baby goat named Dean came to live at Rancho Relaxo, a nonprofit rescue farm, around the same time as Michael, a Great Pyrenees. Michael was brought to the farm to help protect all of the smaller animals there, and he and Dean had an instant connection. Dean isn't deterred by their difference in size. In fact, some of Dean's first friends on the farm were the horses. He would prance around their field, and they were very gentle with this new little kid. Now the feisty little goat likes head-butting Michael, teasing him, and trying to get him to play. He'll bleat and he'll baa, he'll run and he'll hop. Then, at the end of each day, the two press pause on their playtime to snuggle up together to go to sleep. They have a very sweet, funny dynamic. "Dean is definitely the star and Michael is his sidekick," says Caitlin Cimini, the farm's owner. "Dean steals the show—always. But Michael doesn't mind at all."

CHEETAH AND PUPPY: FRIENDS FOR LIFE

LOCATION: WINSTON, OREGON, U.S.A.

When a new cheetah cub named Pancake was born at the Wildlife Safari in Oregon, the staff knew she needed a friend for life. So they adopted a Rhodesian ridgeback puppy named Dayo who was born on the exact same day. This particular breed is a good match for cheetahs because the dogs have very similar life spans (13 to 15 years) and grow to be about the same size at around 80 to 100 pounds (36 to 45 kg). And they both love to run—though a pup will never be quite as fast! Having a dog around ensures that Pancake won't be lonely, sad, or anxious, and that she'll get lots of playtime. Pancake and Dayo instantly got along, with Dayo following Pancake all around. They wrestle together, share toys, nap together, and, of course, run together! While a dog might not be the most exotic animal in a zoo, Dayo is definitely invaluable to Pancake.

POTBELLIED PIG WINS OVER POOCH

LOCATION: SAN DIEGO, CALIFORNIA, U.S.A.

For this pig and pup pair, theirs was not love at first sight. When Myles the boxer first met Rudy the potbellied pig, he was less than thrilled. In fact, he would run away from the poor piggy whenever Rudy approached him. But little by little, day by day, the two began to grow on each other. Now these two share snacks (their favorite is animal crackers), they snuggle, and they sometimes make mischief—they often join forces to try to avoid wearing sunscreen by running away from their owner, Jordan Russo. These two are such sweet friends that Myles will even dig holes for Rudy to root around in (a favorite activity for pigs). Having grown up around dogs, Rudy now fancies himself one. He's learned to sit for treats, and he insists on being inside the house with the other dogs. "If the door is shut, he will stand outside and squeal until we let him in," says Jordan. "Myles even taught him to use the doggy door." Sometimes, the best friendships are worth waiting for!

SCARED GOAT PURSUES PIG

LOCATION: VICTORIA, AUSTRALIA

If ever you're in a new place and feeling unsure, find a friend. That's exactly what a nervous little goat named Tarzan did when he wound up in an Australian animal shelter. He quickly befriended a confident pig named Cheesecake. Everywhere that Cheesecake went, Tarzan went, too. And if ever Cheesecake was out of his sights, Tarzan seemed to get upset and a bit stressed. The two developed a deep bond being in the shelter together, and thankfully, they eventually made it to Edgar's Mission animal sanctuary together, where they get to be with each other 24/7. And that's just how they like it! They like to eat from the same food tray (despite the fact that they each have their own), chase each other, and lay in the sun soaking up rays. These two went from the pound to their own personal paradise and stayed pals through it all.

TARZAN

CHEESECAKE

TORTOISE BESTIES

LOCATION: PEORIA, ARIZONA, U.S.A.

These pals are totally rad! Chompers and Littlefoot are two African spurred tortoises (also known as sulcata tortoises). These tortoises can grow to be more than 200 pounds (91 kg) and live more than 100 years. But Chompers is just two years old and Littlefoot is eight months. While it did take a little while for Chompers to warm up to Littlefoot (he'd gotten used to being an only turtle, after all), the two are now the best of friends. These two slow-moving sidekicks even have their own social media account, where they entertain their many fans with incredible antics. Littlefoot likes to skateboard, Chompers enjoys being petted on the head, and together, they roam around the yard, share their food (especially lettuce, strawberries, and bananas), warm themselves in the sun, and even dress up in costumes for the holidays. But their favorite thing to do together? Getting sprayed with the hose. Right on, dude!

THEY CALL ME CHOMPERS FOR A REASON!

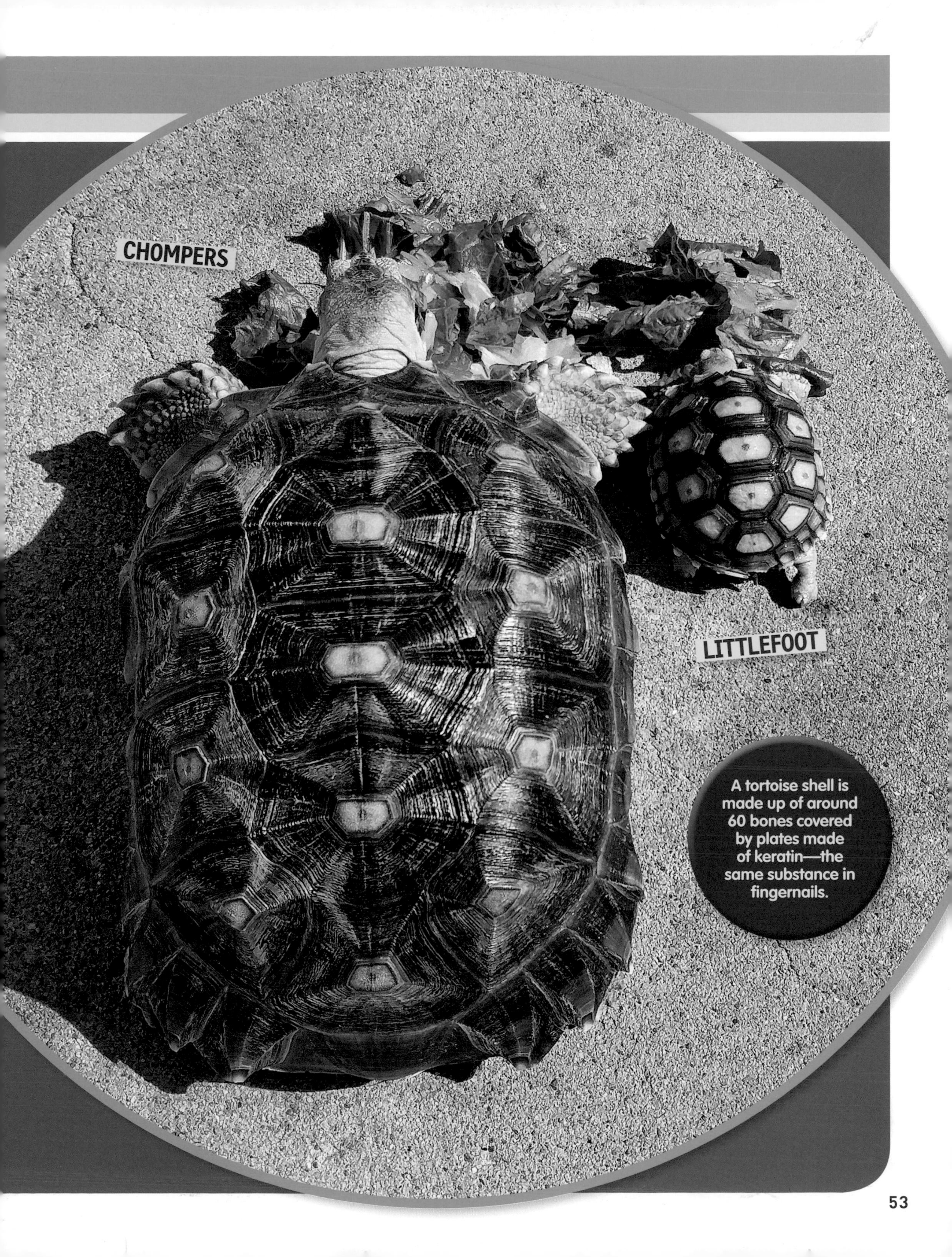

A tortoise shell is made up of around 60 bones covered by plates made of keratin—the same substance in fingernails.

SMALL STALLION AND BOXER BUD

LOCATION: BELLINGHAM, WASHINGTON, U.S.A.

Einstein is a miniature horse. While all miniature horses are small, Einstein is really small. He is practically a mini miniature horse. In fact, at 24 inches (61 cm) tall, he's the world's smallest stallion. He's so small that in order to make sure he doesn't get hurt, he isn't able to play with regular-size horses. Instead, he has befriended his owner's boxer, Lilly. Lilly is a sweet, patient pup who's much closer to Einstein in size and who never leaves his side. The pair might be small, but their big personalities have won them tons of adoring fans— Lilly and Einstein have appeared in newspapers, on TV, and even have their own book! These days the two spend their time chasing each other, playing together, and going into town to pick up their fan mail.

BRAVE BIRD LOVES BIG DOG

LOCATION: McFARLAND, WISCONSIN, U.S.A.

Merlin, a green-cheeked conure, is a very brave bird. His best friend is Nola, a large mixed-breed dog! Merlin climbs all over Nola—on his head, on his back, between his legs—and Nola seems pretty unbothered by being his feathered friend's jungle gym. Merlin even takes up-close-and-personal one step further by nibbling on Nola's cheeks and eyes, and even sometimes trying to clean his teeth! Merlin's so trusting of Nola that he will nestle under the dog's head while he's eating a bone. While Nola is rambunctious and energetic with other dogs, he is gentle and patient with Merlin. Merlin so loves being around the sweet pup that his owner got him a special little bird harness so that the two can lounge outside together. How tweet!

Small birds in the wild will often clean the teeth of large animals.

DOG'S BEST FRIEND? A CAT!

CHARLIE

DOUG

LOCATION: GUERNEVILLE, CALIFORNIA, U.S.A.

Teresa Tuffli and her husband rescued Doug the cat just a few months before they rescued Charlie, a golden retriever puppy. Both were about 13 pounds (5.9 kg) and a very similar color. You would have thought these two were twins, if it weren't for the fact that they were different species. So, it's probably safe to assume that at the very least, they thought they were brothers! Right away, these two had a super special connection. Anywhere Charlie went, Doug was sure to go. If Charlie hopped up on the couch, so did Doug. If Charlie laid down for a nap, so did Doug. Now that Charlie has grown into his more-than-70-pound (31.8-kg) self, he and Doug are still two peas in a pod. They sleep together (Doug loves to lay in the spot between Charlie's front and back leg), take turns drinking from Charlie's water bowl together, and snuggle together (Doug loves burying his face in Charlie's soft, floppy ears). And some days, after Doug eats, Charlie will lick his face to groom him. For sweet Doug, who loves his Charlie so, these are the best days.

DOG SNUGGLES SQUIRREL

LOCATION: PASADENA, CALIFORNIA, U.S.A.

When Stewart was a baby squirrel, he fell out of a tree. Someone found him, and when they weren't able to find his mother, they brought him into a veterinarian's office. Unfortunately, the vet wasn't able to take care of the little guy, so Kendall Smith volunteered. She brought Stewart home to live with her and her dog, Callie, a miniature Australian shepherd. Kendall nursed Stewart back to health, feeding him goat's milk with a tiny eyedropper. She was confident that Callie would be gentle with little Stewart because the sweet pup had met several other small animals in the past. Sure enough, Stewart and Callie bonded right away, with Stewart cuddling up against Callie for warmth and snuggling in her soft fur. Today, Stewart is healthy and happy, eats his favorite foods (bananas and walnuts), climbs all over Callie, and runs laps around the house with Callie until one of them gets tuckered out—usually Callie! These pals are nuts about each other!

Callie is so gentle that she's even a therapy dog for a student in the special education class Kendall teaches.

GOAT OPPOSITES ATTRACT

LOCATION: MAPLE VALLEY, WASHINGTON, U.S.A.

Sometimes, opposites attract. Gunner, a very big goat, was brought to the Puget Sound Goat Rescue after being rescued from a sad, lonely life where he was kept all alone in a pen. He didn't have experience being around other goats, and while he was much bigger than them, he was terrified of them. Around the same time, a very little goat named Buster came to the farm. He wasn't adjusting well to being in a big group, either. He was scared, too. So, the owner of the farm, Barbara Jamison, put the two nervous goats together. And wouldn't you know it, they've been inseparable ever since. "We have tried several times to put Buster back in with goat kids his own age, but he just cries and cries," says Barbara. "And we have tried to integrate giant Gunner into the adult herd, and even though he outweighs them all by many pounds, he is just terrified to be with them. So, it looks like they are a team."

WE ARE A PRETTY ADORABLE TEAM, INDEED!

CAT CLIMBS OVER PATIENT PIG

LOCATION: MEMPHIS, TENNESSEE, U.S.A.

One day, Anna Key was riding her bike when she found a tiny kitten abandoned in a pile of trash. She immediately picked her up to bring her home. Her only concern was how her potbellied pig, Ella, would react to this adorable little ball of fur. Ella had gotten very used to being the queen of the castle. She likes to be pampered with fluffy blankets, soft pillows, and lots of snuggles. But as it turns out, there was nothing to worry about! The two animals bonded straightaway and even took a nap together the first day they met. Now the two snuggle up together, and the cat, whom Anna named Mercy, climbs all over patient Ella, even sitting up on Ella's back for the ultimate piggyback ride.

FAMOUS FRIENDS

Run into these friends on the street and you may want to ask for a slobbery selfie, or at the very least a paw-tograph!

PANDA TWINS TAKE WORLD BY STORM

LOCATION: ATLANTA, GEORGIA, U.S.A.

It's pretty awesome having a best friend. It's even more awesome when that best friend is your brother or sister! You get to spend lots of time together, you can chat about your parents, and you don't have to go home to separate houses after you've been hanging out! That's exactly what it's like for baby giant panda twins Ya Lun (*Ya* means "elegant" in Chinese) and Xi Lun (*Xi* means "happy" in Chinese). These sisters were born at Zoo Atlanta in September 2016. Now they spend their days sharing an enclosure, climbing, wrestling, and perhaps the cutest, snuggling up together when they take naps. The best part is, you can watch them on the zoo's PandaCam, 24 hours a day!

BO AND SUNNY, PRESIDENTIAL PUPS

LOCATION: WASHINGTON, D.C., U.S.A.

When President Barack Obama won the election in 2008, he had to make good on many promises he made during his campaign. But perhaps his cutest, cuddliest promise was one he made to his daughters, Sasha and Malia. He promised that after the election, the family could finally get a dog, which the girls had wanted for a long time. And that they did! A Portuguese water dog named Bo joined the first family and became a presidential pooch. Bo loved his family and daily routines, but the White House is a big place—he needed a friend to share his home! So the Obama family got a second dog of the same breed and named her Sunny. Bo and Sunny were super popular with visitors to the White House, and they attended many events, like the Easter Egg Roll, Take Your Child to Work Day, and holiday festivities. The dogs loved to romp around on the South Lawn, play in the snow, and play catch with the president—and, of course, they took their jobs as First Dogs very seriously!

Portuguese water dogs have a waterproof coat and were historically trained to help fishers along the coast of Portugal.

DOG AND CAT GO HIKING

LOCATION: MARBELLA, SPAIN

These two cuties are famous for not only their awesome adventures, but their furry friendship as well! According to owners Sebastian and Finn, Bandito the pug and Luigi the cat get along like most siblings do. "They can start sudden whirlwinds of activity—chasing each other or chasing the same toy," says Sebastian. "Then the next minute they'll be curled up asleep." But these sweet "siblings" are also pretty unique—not only have they traveled more than most pets, they've traveled more than many humans! Together with their owners, these four-legged adventurers hiked Spain's 497-mile (800-km) Camino de Santiago trail. To take the journey, Sebastian and Finn got a special pet stroller so that Bandito and Luigi could rest when they got tired, and at night the family of four would sleep together in a tent. "They're so close," says Sebastian. "They're like soul mates in a way." And during their down time, the duo poses for adorable videos for their many fans on social media. This little dog-and-cat pair have it figured out—it's always better traveling with a friend!

DOG AND CATS FOSTER KITTENS

SUZIE

SUNNY KUSHI

LOCATION: OCEAN CITY, NEW JERSEY, U.S.A.

When Kelly began fostering kittens, her adopted boxer, Suzie, became calmer and more content. Taking on a motherly role with the kittens gave Suzie a job and a purpose. Then, Kelly adopted two special needs cats—Kushi and Sunny. Both of the cats have trouble seeing, but that definitely doesn't seem to slow them down. Kushi and Sunny chase each other around the house at full speed, climb, and jump. Sure, there's a fair amount of crashing into things, but they're very happy being able to live full, feisty lives together. "They have a grand old time," says Kelly. "I think maybe they provide a bit of confidence and encouragement to one another." These three buds sleep near one another, hang out together, share toys (Suzie likes catnip and the kittens love the pup's dirty tennis ball), and drink out of one another's water bowls. Amazingly, they also work together to help with the kittens Kelly fosters. "They each have their specific roles and duties," says Kelly. "They get very concerned when they hear crying kittens and all want to help. Suzie snuggles them, Kushi grooms them, and Sunny plays with them."

A HORSE, MINI HORSE, AND DONKEY TEAM UP

LOCATION: GOSHEN, KENTUCKY, U.S.A.

These "three musketeers" live together in one stall, eat together, go for walks together, and, of course, play together! The leader of the pack is Lionus, a big Canadian horse with an even bigger personality and heart. He loves participating in competitions, befriending other animals, and being silly (he loves smiling for treats). When Lionus met Oreo, an 11-year-old miniature horse, Oreo was in serious need of a friend. He was living at a farm where none of the other horses were very nice to him. But while the other horses turned their backs on Oreo, Lionus welcomed him with open hooves. Lionus and Oreo began spending their days together, and before long Oreo became like Lionus's little shadow. Lionus loves his little Oreo so much he even lets him take cover beneath his big body when it rains. But their friendship wasn't quite complete: A few years later, the duo became a trio with the addition of Bamboo, or Boo for short. Lionus and Oreo's owner, Alison Otter, bought the miniature donkey to keep Oreo company while Lionus was off traveling for horse shows. Together, these three pals form an unstoppable team!

DOG LOVES RAT

LOCATION: NEW YORK, NEW YORK, U.S.A.

Even though Cooper is a coonhound (which is a hunting breed), he couldn't be more gentle and sweet with his funny buddy, Olivia the rat. Right when they met, Cooper began licking Olivia, who was immediately enamored with the sweet pup. She began following him around everywhere, and just like that, a bond was formed. These two spunky sweeties like playing outside in the backyard together, but their owner, Chris Durham, never has to worry about losing little Olivia. He just says "Where's the rat?" and Cooper uses his super sniffer to find her right away. Another favorite game the two like to play is when Olivia burrows under blankets inside the house and Cooper digs her out. While definitely a very surprising pairing, these two couldn't be cuter.

DANTE

LUCA

LOCATION: ROSE HILL, KANSAS, U.S.A.

When Dante showed up at Benediction Farm, no one was quite sure where he came from, but the tiny kitten seemed to have a plan of his own. It was a cold and rainy day, and Dante was only eight weeks old and soaking wet. "The farmers opened the door and this tiny, wet kitten marched in and just sat down," says Rupa Sutton. From there, this social little guy started making friends all around the farm, including with Rupa's 12-year-old Friesian horse, Luca. The moment they saw each other, they started nuzzling and cuddling—something they still do to this day when they see each other. Luca even gives Dante massages with his upper lip, which this friendly feline loves! Dante has no fear when it comes to horses, and he'll kiss them and nuzzle them. He's even ridden one once! Dante also loves riding in the hay cart from one barn to the other. It seems like Dante knew just what he was doing when he picked this farm on that cold, rainy day!

HORSE IS SMITTEN FOR KITTEN

DOG SNUGGLES WITH CAMEL

LOCATION: VICTORIA, AUSTRALIA

When Alana the camel arrived at Bellevue Farmstay in Australia, she was just hours old. Alana's mother couldn't feed her, so the owners of Bellevue, Warren and Wendy Couch, took her in and began bottle-feeding her. But the humans weren't the only ones taken by this camel cutie—so were two of their dogs: Nikki, a golden retriever, and Tess, a border collie. Right away, Nikki began mothering Alana and even trying to keep other animals away from her. It took Alana about three weeks to get steady on her legs, but before that, the animals would lie together in the yard and Alana would crawl over to steal carrots from the dogs' mouths. The sweet dogs and the camel calf even started curling up together at the end of the day and sharing a bed. Now that Alana has grown and lives outside with the other farm animals, she still has a special place in her heart for her pup pals and visits with them often. Alana has learned to give visitors kisses and even tries to round up the cows, which is something she's seen her buddy Tess, a trained cattle dog, do. These three are one happy farm family.

BOXER TRAINS BULLDOG

LOCATION: LOUISVILLE, KENTUCKY, U.S.A.

Lindley and Chad Turner had a dog they adored—a well-behaved boxer named Lyle—and weren't really in the market for a new pup. But when Lindley found out there was a dog in need of a loving home, she decided to at least meet her. What Lindley found was a nervous and lonely English bulldog. "The first time I met her, she jumped up on me and gave me one of her bulldog hugs," says Lindley. And that's all it took. Lindley brought her home and named her Dolly. While Dolly is a dog with a heart of gold, she was also a bit of a wild woman. She took flying leaps off of furniture, jumped, barked, and chewed on everything. Lindley and Chad did their best to train her. But what they soon saw in the months that followed was that Lyle was teaching her, too! At first, Dolly would go wild in the car, get out of control when she played, and become super nervous and destroy things when Lindley and Chad left the house. But over time, Lyle showed her how to lie down and relax in the car, how to play nice, and that when their humans went away, they would come back. Now when they leave, Dolly doesn't even follow them to the door anymore—she just goes and lies beside Lyle on his bed. Lyle and Dolly have become playmates, partners in crime, and—sweetest of all—best friends.

THE DYNAMIC DUO, THAT'S US!

DOG AND CAT ATTEND PUPPY BOWL

OSCAR

All of the animals featured in the Puppy Bowl are available for adoption.

LOCATION: PHOENIX, ARIZONA, U.S.A.

What's better than being a sporty superstar? Having a lifelong friend! As fate would have it, Roxy, a Chihuahua/French bulldog mix, and Oscar, an American shorthair cat, were both rescued around the same time by the Arizona Humane Society and placed in the same foster home. There they became the best of buds—wrestling, sharing toys, playing hide-and-seek, and curling up together for naps. These two made each other so happy that when Roxy was asked to participate in the Puppy Bowl (a spoof of the Super Bowl in which football players are swapped for puppies), Oscar went with her. Together they flew from Arizona to New York City and had the adventure of a lifetime. Roxy took pictures in Central Park, in Times Square, in a taxi, and so much more. While Roxy was a little overwhelmed at the actual game (she kept running into the corner when they'd put her on the field), she loved going back to the hotel, where she could romp around with her best bud and number one fan, Oscar. But the most exciting, happiest part of their journey was when they returned to Arizona and found out that they both were adopted and would be going home soon—together!

DOG GETS PET GUINEA PIG

LOCATION: VANCOUVER, BRITISH COLUMBIA, CANADA

It's not every day that a pet gets a pet of their own. But that's exactly what Sunshade, an adorable Airedale terrier, got. Every week his owner would take him to the pet store and he would stand in front of the guinea pig cages, just watching the furry critters. And one day, after years of waiting patiently, Sunshade's owner Elaine Hu got him his own guinea pig named Meatball! At first Sunshade was so excited, his owners were nervous to put the guinea pig down in case he might hurt her. But when they did, they saw how sweet and gentle the dog was with his new friend. They soon got another guinea pig, Sesame, and then Meatball had three babies! Sunshade took his role as protector and nurturer of the baby guinea pigs very seriously. He licked them and snuggled them and happily let them crawl all over him. Sunshade was as happy as could be—he went from wishing for a guinea pig to having five in less than a year, and oh how he loved them all.

SUNSHADE

TWIN GOATS ARE BORN BESTIES

LOCATION: ANNANDALE, NEW JERSEY, U.S.A.

Lyla and Chibs are twin goats who prove that siblings can really be the greatest of friends. Both goats had a rough start in life. Lyla was born with just three legs, and Chibs was born with contracted tendons in his legs that he needed surgery to fix. Luckily, the two besties were both rescued from a farm in Kentucky and now live happily together at Goats of Anarchy™. They are completely inseparable and like to be by each other's side 24/7. Chibs is Lyla's protector, and he even taught her how to play. Whenever they are apart, they call to each other until they can be reunited. With these sweet siblings, the snuggle is real.

CHIBS

LYLA

TWINS HAVE DOUBLE THE FUN!

MORRIS THE HORSE-RIDING CAT

LOCATION: NORTHERN NEW SOUTH WALES, AUSTRALIA

When rescue cat Morris went home with his owner, Jennifer Boyle, he was a little nervous to meet all of her horses. Morris had never met a horse, and they were much, much bigger than him. But one of Jennifer's horses in particular, Champy, was smitten with the little kitten. And when Morris finally warmed up to Champy, the cat even let the horse use his big teeth to groom him! Then one day, Morris jumped onto Champy's back and a best friendship was born. Pretty soon, Morris started grooming Champy's mane and tail—a true sign of trust and affection. Now the feisty feline will go for hours-long rides on the sweet horse's back (but only when Champy's wearing a blanket so Morris doesn't slide off), and Champy will even sidle up to wherever Morris is standing to coax him on. Giddyup!

THE CATS AND THE RATS

LOCATION: ORLANDO, FLORIDA, U.S.A.

When you think of animal friends, cats and rats might not be the first pair that come to mind! But Loraine De Souza's critter crew proves that with love, anything is possible. When Loraine brought her three new kittens—Willow, Lucifer, and Fabio—home, she took each of her four rats—Stella, Merla, Mishka, and Mila—out of their cages for an introduction. Instantly, they accepted one another. "My kittens and rats love to play together all the time," says Loraine. "Whenever the cats pass the rats' cage, they stick their noses in and the rats come running to them and try to pull their noses in with their hands." The rats and their feline friends love to play by chasing one another, and the cats love climbing into the rats' cage. The rats also enjoy eating treats (like salads and snack puffs) and licking the cats' noses. As for the cats, as soon as they hear Loraine opening the rats' cage door, they come running. This game of cat and mouse has a very happy ending!

CHIMP HELPS INJURED FRIEND

LOCATION: FORT PIERCE, FLORIDA, U.S.A.

Ursula and Rebel are two chimpanzees who were rescued after having spent years being used as subjects for medical research. Today, they live together at the Save the Chimps animal sanctuary in Fort Pierce, Florida. A few years ago, Rebel had an injury and was temporarily paralyzed. But after receiving great medical treatment and physical therapy, he is almost completely back to his old self. But since then, the caretakers at Save the Chimps have noticed that Rebel has become something of a caretaker for other sick or injured chimps—especially for Ursula. Ursula lost the use of her back legs because of a disease in her lower back. She moves around by scooting or pulling herself with straps and ramps built just for her. Rebel is sensitive to Ursula's situation and has begun to follow her, sit next to her to keep her company, and groom her. When Ursula got stronger and started going outside again, Rebel was right there by her side. "He carefully watched over her," says Dr. Jocelyn Bezner, Save the Chimps' senior veterinarian. "When Ursula needed to rest, Rebel sat patiently next to her waiting for her to move, sometimes with his arm around her shoulder." What a great friend!

URSULA

REBEL

Chimps groom each other to relax and socialize.

PIT BULL HELPS SAVE SICK GOAT

GP

PIPER

LOCATION: TULSA, OKLAHOMA, U.S.A.

When GP the goat and his two sisters were born at Julie Free's home, she didn't think she was going to be able to save him. He wasn't responding like his sisters, and he was unwell. So she brought the tiny goat into her house and put him on a towel in the middle of the floor. When she finally let her curious pit bull mix, Piper, near GP, the pup began inspecting the little baby and then licking him. Her licks helped him, and he began moving! Ever since then, the two have had an unbreakable bond. GP follows close behind Piper, and if the motherly pup gets too far from him, he bleats to let everyone know he's unhappy. They run together, play together, and snuggle, and GP (which stands for Goat Puppy) even accompanied Piper to her classes to be a companion animal. They're a mismatch made in heaven!

BABYSITTING BUDS

Animals are pretty incredible; when one sees another in need of a mother, they'll often step in to help—no questions asked. These stories are incredible examples of how a mother's love knows no bounds.

BETH

DOG STEPS IN FOR LION CUBS

LOCATION: CULLINAN, SOUTH AFRICA

Beth the mastiff/Rhodesian ridgeback mix lives at the Horseback Africa animal farm, a center that provides wildlife experiences in South Africa. Shortly after Beth arrived, her motherly instincts kicked in around a pride of 12 lion cubs. She was unfazed by the fact that these little ones were kings of the jungle—or maybe princes, at this point! She began approaching them, licking them, cleaning them, snuggling them, and even reprimanding them when they misbehaved. Beth isn't afraid to run, play, and wrestle with the cubs, who are learning survival skills at the center. The hope is that when these endangered cats get older and ready, they'll be released into the wild. Until then, Beth is the best nanny a little lion prince could ask for.

GOAT RAISES BABY HORSE

LOCATION: COLDWATER, ONTARIO, CANADA

The day after a Clydesdale named Legacy was born, her mother passed away, sadly. Legacy's owners, Emily and Matt Welsh, were heartbroken for the loss of their beloved horse and also very scared for Legacy's well-being. Legacy needed food, and now that her mother was gone, they would have to find another way to get it to her. They tried to find another horse in the area that had recently had a baby and could also feed Legacy, but there weren't any. But then, their farrier (a professional who puts shoes on horses) had an idea: a dairy goat! Before long, a little goat named Buttercup arrived at the farm. Emily and Matt made a ramp for the goat to stand on so that they could milk her more easily. This would also give Legacy the opportunity to feed directly from Buttercup if she wanted to, and—amazingly—she did! Buttercup not only fed Legacy like her mother would have, she still protects her, plays with her, nurtures her, and loves her. Mom of the Year award goes to Buttercup!

Clydesdale horses are one of the largest breeds in the world.

DOG TAKES CARE OF KITTENS

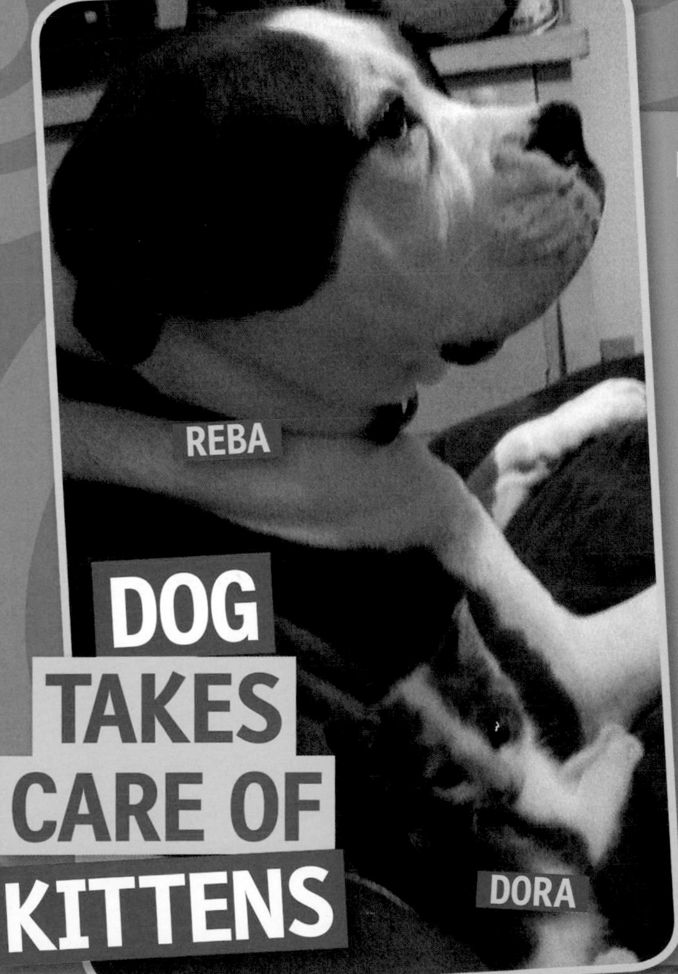

LOCATION: LOUISVILLE, KENTUCKY, U.S.A.

When your office is located inside a barn, you get used to hearing lots of animal noises. But on this particular day, Lindley Beckman Turner heard a noise she wasn't used to—a tiny, persistent mew. When she followed the noise, Lindley found a teeny-tiny newborn kitten. Figuring the kitten must have come from the hayloft, Lindley returned the kitten to where she hoped her mom would be. But a few minutes later, Lindley heard the kitten's cries again. This little furball wanted Lindley's attention, and she wasn't going to give up! Lindley climbed into the hayloft to figure out what was going on. There she discovered the mama cat was long gone and she'd left behind two very hungry kittens. When Lindley brought the two little kittens home to take care of them, she was worried how the kittens would fare without their mother. But no worries—Lindley's sweet boxer pup, Reba, stepped in to save the day. The gentle, loving Reba cuddled the kittens, licked them, and loved them as if they were her own. Today, the two kittens, Dora and Diega, rule the roost at Lindley's parents' home, where they live full-time. Reba gave these now happy and healthy kitties the greatest gift: a loving start to their lives.

DOG RESCUES LOST FAWN

ARE YOU MY MUMMY?

MISHKA

LOCATION: OLYMPIA, WASHINGTON, U.S.A.

Mishka is a Karelian bear dog employed by the Washington State Department of Fish and Wildlife. Mishka is trained to track down bears and cougars that have come too close to where humans are—like shops, neighborhoods, or even schools. First, he finds the animals, and then he chases them toward officers who can capture and relocate them to a place where they are at a safe distance from humans. But while Mishka has a sometimes scary job, it turns out he's a big softie with a heart of gold. One day while Mishka was on the job, he encountered an adorable baby deer, or fawn, who had lost its mother. The fawn quickly mistook Mishka for his mom and wouldn't leave his side. The fawn nuzzled Mishka and followed him everywhere he went. Until the fawn was taken to someone to care for him, sweet Mishka was patient and warm with the lost little young'un, licking his face and snuggling him. Mishka is a great friend—and employee!

PEACOCK BEFRIENDS BUNNIES

LOCATION: ST. LOUIS, MISSOURI, U.S.A.

When Page Pardo rescued Pete the peacock, he was the biggest bird on her farm. At first she was worried that he might bully the smaller birds. Instead, Pete was terrified of them. The first time he went outside to explore the farm, he ran right back inside the barn to hide. To keep him safe at night, Page trained Pete to sleep inside the chicken house with some of the smaller chickens. Pete did make some friends inside that chicken coop, just not with the chickens! Instead, he befriended three giant rescue bunnies. Right off the bat, neither the bunnies nor Pete showed any fear toward the other. Even now that Page has brought some more peacocks onto the farm, the bunnies and the peacocks have remained friends. They hang out together in the chicken coop, and they also stick together outside in the big yard. "I'm not exactly sure what brought about this odd friendship," says Page. "But the peacocks like the bunnies, and the bunnies like them." And that's that!

DOG GUARDS KITTEN

LOCATION: HOLLYWOOD, FLORIDA, U.S.A.

One day, Lorrie Rivera was out walking her 10-year-old dog, Lily (who'd been a gift from her daughter to help guard her flower shop), when they heard the faintest of mews. Before Lorrie could locate the cute little culprit, Lily had the tiny kitten in her mouth, gently holding her like a mother cat would. Lorrie contacted the Humane Society, but they weren't able to take her in for another month. So Lorrie kept the tiny kitten, fed her from a bottle, and figured she would have to really work to keep Lily, a 90-pound (40.8-kg) Japanese Akita, away from the tiny ball of fur. But what happened next surprised her. Lily began treating the kitten as if she were her own. She snuggled her, played with her, and would even alert Lorrie when the kitten was ready to be fed, watching closely to make sure it was done correctly. One thing's for sure: This guard dog has a heart of gold.

Male peafowls are called peacocks, and females are called peahens.

TORTOISE TAKES IN HIPPO

LOCATION: MOMBASA, KENYA, AFRICA

When Owen the hippo was a baby, he was separated from his family by a tsunami. Fortunately, he was rescued and taken to the Haller Park wildlife sanctuary in Kenya. But Owen couldn't stay with the park's other hippos because they wouldn't accept the little guy. As a last resort, the park staff decided to put him in an enclosure with a 130-year-old tortoise named Mzee. In need of a friend after his ordeal, Owen followed Mzee everywhere. At first Mzee wasn't so sure about this new young'un, but Owen kept at it, and soon enough, the two were great pals. Owen even started behaving like a tortoise, eating the same foods Mzee ate and sleeping at night instead of during the day like most hippos. And while tortoises aren't known for their social behavior, Mzee sure seemed to like his happy hippo friend. The two ate leaves together, went for swims together, and took naps together. Mzee would even stretch out his neck so Owen could lick him.

PIG LEADS PACK OF PUPS

LOCATION: CASTROVILLE, TEXAS, U.S.A.

When Shelby Madere first brought Chowder home, he wasn't quite sure what to make of his new family. Shelby knew she was going to have to work extra hard to get the Vietnamese potbellied pig comfortable with her canine crew (and vice versa). Every day Shelby brought Chowder out to play with the dogs. She would supervise and make sure that no one was being picked on. It took Chowder a full year before he enjoyed snuggling or being petted by Shelby, but it wasn't long before Chowder and the pups became great friends. James, a black shepherd, is particularly smitten with Chowder. Every morning James unleashes loads of kisses on Chowder. The 190-pound (86.2-kg) pig also loves to relax in his personal swimming pool while the dogs run around him. Chowder loves lying in the sun with the dogs, sleeping with them, and curling up with them in front of the fire at night.

One of Chowder's favorite toys is a water bottle filled with frozen peas. As Chowder pushes the bottle around with his snout, the peas fall out, giving him a tasty treat.

CAT IS A NURSE!

RADEMENES

LOCATION: BYDGOSZCZ, POLAND

When he was just a tiny kitten, Rademenes was diagnosed with an infection in his lungs known as an inflamed respiratory tract. But the sweet little fighter overcame his illness and has since found a remarkable purpose. Amazingly, once Rademenes regained his strength, he began comforting the other sick and recovering animals at the Polish animal shelter where he was treated. Today, he's become a permanent resident there and is so good at his job that they've taken to calling him "Cat Nurse." Rademenes will snuggle up to a sick dog or cat to bring comfort and warmth. He'll nap with them, lick them, and even wrap his little paws around their body in a loving, furry hug. What a pal!

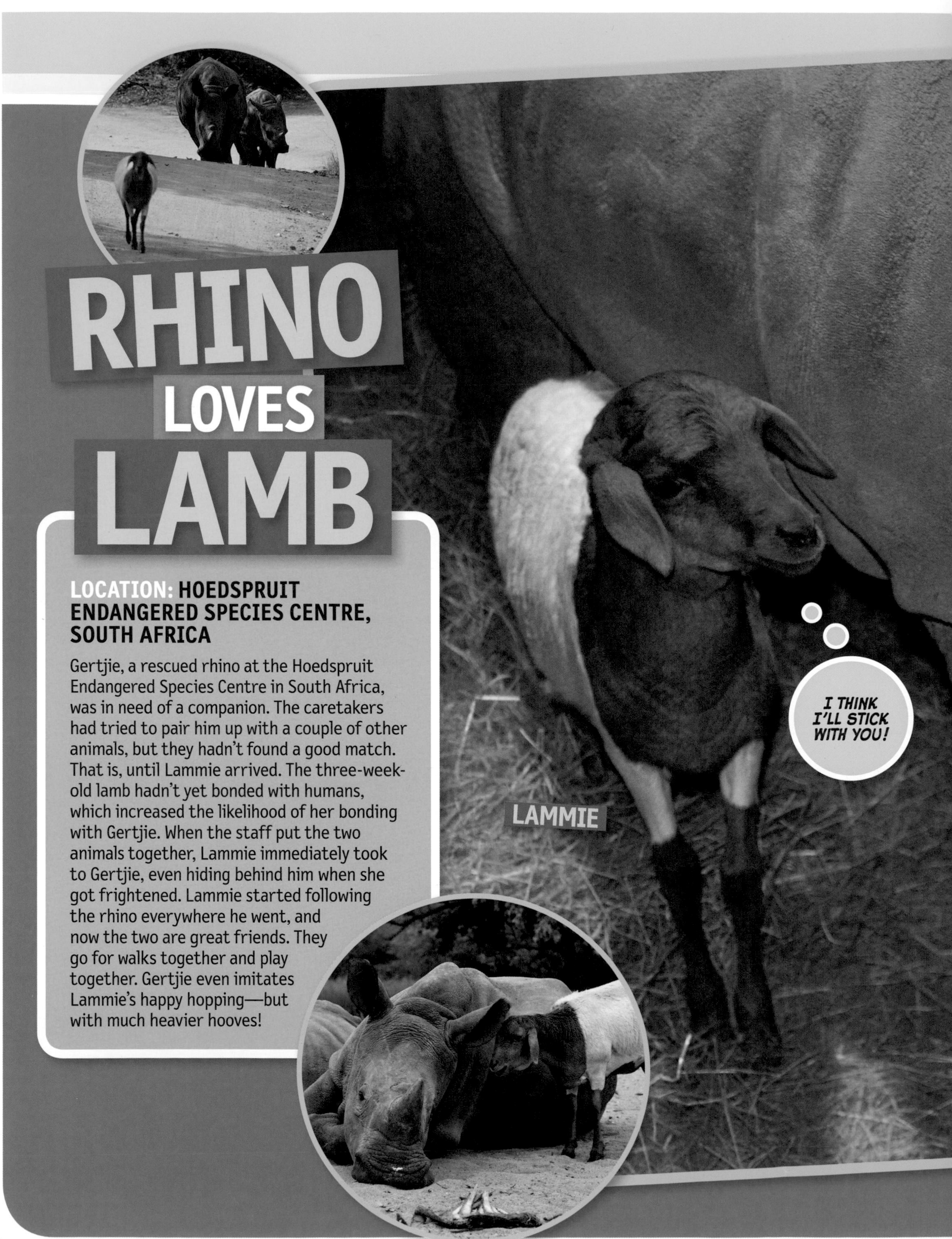

RHINO LOVES LAMB

LOCATION: HOEDSPRUIT ENDANGERED SPECIES CENTRE, SOUTH AFRICA

Gertjie, a rescued rhino at the Hoedspruit Endangered Species Centre in South Africa, was in need of a companion. The caretakers had tried to pair him up with a couple of other animals, but they hadn't found a good match. That is, until Lammie arrived. The three-week-old lamb hadn't yet bonded with humans, which increased the likelihood of her bonding with Gertjie. When the staff put the two animals together, Lammie immediately took to Gertjie, even hiding behind him when she got frightened. Lammie started following the rhino everywhere he went, and now the two are great friends. They go for walks together and play together. Gertjie even imitates Lammie's happy hopping—but with much heavier hooves!

A rhinoceros's horn is made out of keratin, the same material our hair and fingernails are made from.

DOG BOTTLE-FEEDS SHEEP

LOCATION: DEVON, ENGLAND, U.K.

When a springer spaniel named Jess was just a few weeks old, her owner, Louise Moorhouse, taught her how to hold a bottle of milk in her mouth. The owner of a large sheep farm in England, Louise knew that this was a skill that would come in quite, erm, handy! Sweet Jess runs through fields with the bottle in her mouth, feeding lambs whose mothers can't care for them. She stands and waits patiently as a little lamb finishes eating and then she heads off to feed the next hungry mouth. Jess takes her work very seriously, and rain or shine, she makes her rounds three times a day. Always one to be helpful, Jess can also carry buckets of feed in her mouth for older sheep. It's safe to say she is beloved by her fluffy family!

CAT COMFORTS BABY OWL

LOCATION: PANAMA CITY, PANAMA

When Ileana (who works rescuing and rehabilitating owls) received Moonlight, an abandoned owl just a few days old, she knew she had a lot of work ahead of her. Because Moonlight didn't have any feathers yet, Ileana had to watch his body temperature closely all through the day and night. To make sure he never got too cold, she kept Moonlight in a special room, used heat lamps to keep him warm, and gave him a plush owl toy that he snuggled under just like he would if he were still with his owl mom. While Ileana was taking care of little Moonlight, her two-year-old Siamese cat, Lulú, was watching and growing more comfortable with the baby owl. Lulú had met other owls that Ileana rescued, but had never seemed quite so interested in one. Lulú would gently place her paw on Moonlight as if to give him comfort, and Lulú began eating little bits of food from Moonlight's plate. Before long the two were hanging out together like two old friends. Lulú seems to think Moonlight is fascinating and funny. But there is one thing Lulú doesn't find amusing—when Moonlight grabs her tail!

MOONLIGHT

LULÚ

GUINEA PIG PICKS DOG

MILO

STUART

LOCATION: TRAVERSE CITY, MICHIGAN, U.S.A.

Milo the golden retriever and Stuart the guinea pig are two sweeties who have become best friends. When Milo was just about a year and a half old, Kristin Hooper brought home Stuart, who was just a baby at the time. Ever since then, they've been like brothers. In fact, Kristin says they haven't quite figured out they're not the same species. They snack on broccoli together, spend time together outside (Stuart eats the grass while Milo plays fetch), and will even curl up in a crate together. The two furry friends like to hang out under the dinner table while their human family eats, ready to clean up any crumbs that might fall. Stuart also loves being groomed. He gets frequent haircuts to manage his long mane, and Milo loves to look on and supervise. The sweet dog will sit and just observe as Stuart gets bathed and coiffed. Stuart might be a guinea pig, but Milo thinks he is top dog.

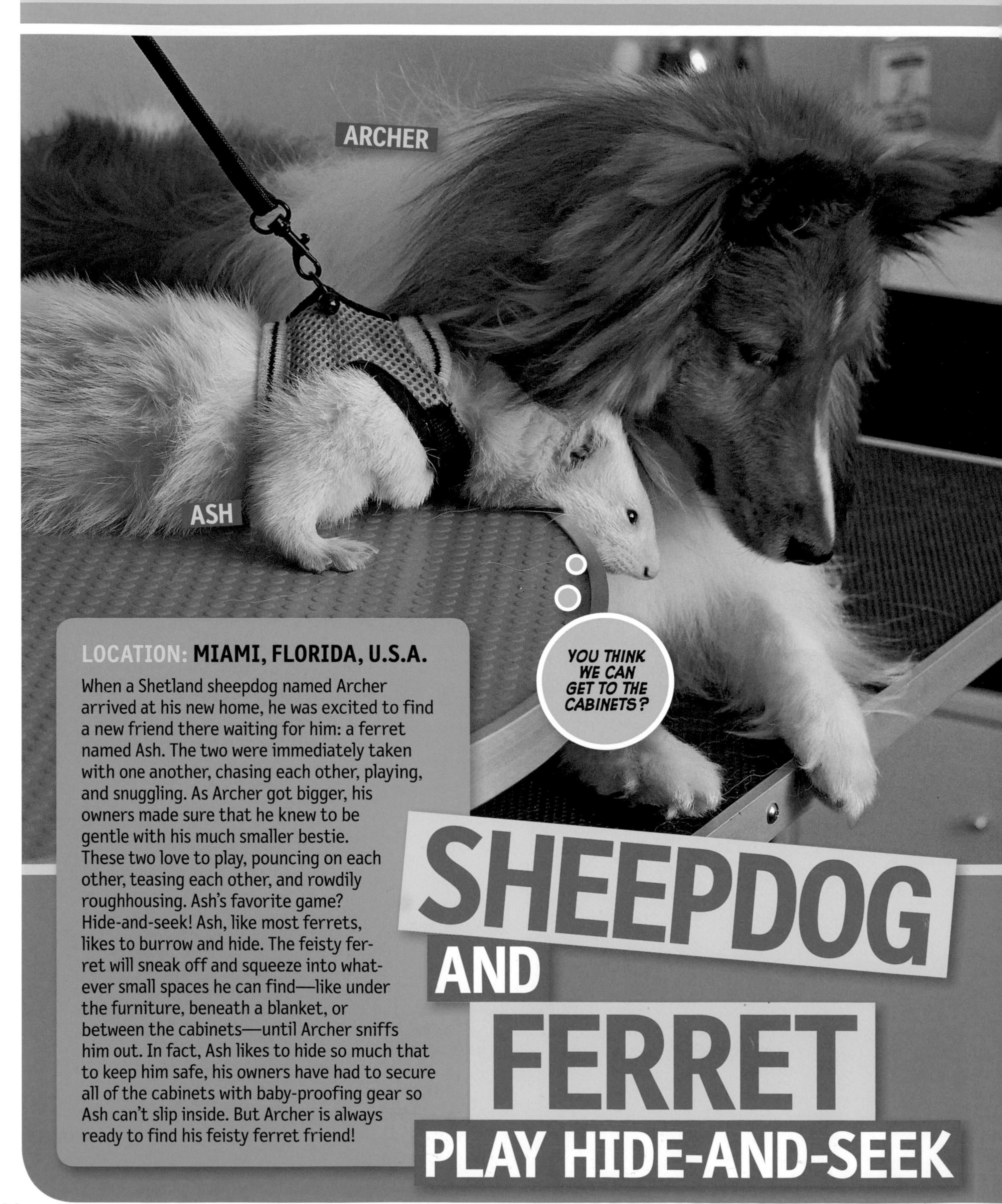

SHEEPDOG AND FERRET PLAY HIDE-AND-SEEK

LOCATION: MIAMI, FLORIDA, U.S.A.

When a Shetland sheepdog named Archer arrived at his new home, he was excited to find a new friend there waiting for him: a ferret named Ash. The two were immediately taken with one another, chasing each other, playing, and snuggling. As Archer got bigger, his owners made sure that he knew to be gentle with his much smaller bestie. These two love to play, pouncing on each other, teasing each other, and rowdily roughhousing. Ash's favorite game? Hide-and-seek! Ash, like most ferrets, likes to burrow and hide. The feisty ferret will sneak off and squeeze into whatever small spaces he can find—like under the furniture, beneath a blanket, or between the cabinets—until Archer sniffs him out. In fact, Ash likes to hide so much that to keep him safe, his owners have had to secure all of the cabinets with baby-proofing gear so Ash can't slip inside. But Archer is always ready to find his feisty ferret friend!

DONKEYS CHARM HORSE

LOCATION: LA GRANGE, KENTUCKY, U.S.A.

Charlie is an eight-year-old Thoroughbred who has spent most of her life in a busy barn around lots of other horses. But recently, her owners, Diane and Dr. David Beckman, needed to move her to a barn where she would be the only horse. Worried that Charlie would be too lonely there, the Beckmans brought two miniature donkeys, Jack and Rose, to keep her company. But Charlie, who's normally super calm, was terrified of the little animals! She was so scared that the first time she saw them, she started running. But the sweet little donkeys were desperate to be friends with Charlie, and they weren't going to give up so easily! So instead of getting too close when she was scared, they patiently kept their distance. Then, when she calmed down, they'd inch a little closer. Over the next couple of days, the determined donkeys kept at it until, finally, Charlie understood that they came in peace and began to embrace them. Now Charlie loves her two burro besties, and Jack and Rose love having a big horse to protect them.

A horse's height is measured in "hands." One hand is equal to four inches.

CAT AND DOG: ADVENTURE BUDDIES

INFINITY
ROSIE

LOCATION: BAY AREA, CALIFORNIA, U.S.A.

When Thoa Bui first brought home her new cat, Rosie, she was weak and wasn't eating. Thoa wasn't sure Rosie would make it. But when she put Rosie with her Siberian husky Lilo, things started to turn around. Lilo loved Rosie like she was her own. She warmed her and comforted her, and soon Rosie began drinking from a bottle. Now Rosie is big and strong, and these two are inseparable adventure buddies. They love exploring the great outdoors together. Along with their other Siberian husky sister, named Infinity, they go hiking, kayaking, and even paddleboarding! They love to roughhouse and go for car rides. Rosie is so certain she's just one of the pups, she even tries eating their dog food! But Lilo is always watching out for her feline friend. "When we're walking together and Lilo sees a random dog, she uses her body to block Rosie so that she's protected," says Thoa. "And sometimes, when they're sleeping at night, Rosie takes up all the space in Lilo's bed, so she ends up on the floor next to Rosie. It's super cute."

QUIRKY CUTIES

Bring on the LOLs! These funny friends are sure to make you smile. And while they might seem like the ultimate clowns, their sweet stories will warm your heart.

MABEL

I AM MABEL, THE NUMBER ONE NANNY!

HEN ROOSTS ON LITTER OF PUPPIES

LOCATION: SHREWSBURY, ENGLAND, U.K.

When Mabel the hen was injured during an accident with a horse, Edward and Ros Tate decided to have her come live inside the house on their farm in England. When she did, she encountered the family dog's brand-new litter of puppies. Within a few days, the dog, Nettle, was up and about, going outside and doing this and that. And whenever Mabel saw the pups unattended, she would hop on top to keep them warm, just like she would a nest of eggs. When Nettle finally saw this bird roosting on her pups, she wasn't quite sure what to make of it, but soon she got used to it and perhaps even appreciated the help; Mabel certainly made an excellent nanny!

SQUIRREL HIDES NUTS IN DOG'S FUR

LOCATION: PARKVILLE, MARYLAND, U.S.A.

A month after Shannon Apple adopted a Bernese mountain dog named Jax, a friend brought her a baby squirrel that had fallen out of a tree. Not one to turn away an animal in need, Shannon began taking care of the little guy and named him Wally. Right away, Jax loved little Wally, and the sweet squirrel grew up thinking it was perfectly normal to have a huge, hairy, barking big brother. As Wally got a bit bigger, the two began to play more and loved chasing each other around. When they got tired, they'd happily take a rest together on the couch. But then their friendship took a really nutty turn. "One day Wally decided to use Jax's fur to hide his stash of nuts!" says Shannon. Jax would sit patiently as Wally burrowed about in his fur, burying nuts, just like squirrels bury nuts in the dirt or leaves in the wild. "Wally started using anywhere he could find to hide things," she says. "He'd use dog toys, Jax's food bowl, under Jax's bed—even Jax's tail!" These funny friends are nuts for each other!

CHICKEN RIDES CAPYBARA

LOCATION: MIDWAY, ARKANSAS, U.S.A.

Janice Wolf, owner of Rocky Ridge Refuge, has two capybaras (the world's largest rodent). The animals resemble a hairy pig or a beaver without a tail, and can grow to weigh up to 150 pounds (68 kg)! The "capys," Cheesecake and Cobbler, help raise litters of puppies at the animal sanctuary. Cheesecake and Cobbler eat with the puppies, sleep with them, and even try to teach the little ones manners! So Janice wasn't at all worried about how the capys would behave when she introduced them to a flock of chicks. But she was surprised how one of the baby chickens took to *them.* This particular chick, Elvira, is a naked neck, which is a breed of chicken without any feathers on its neck. The chicks had been living in the same area as Cheesecake and Cobbler until one day when Janice moved them into their own pen. But Elvira wasn't too pleased with the new living arrangement, so she flew back to be with the capys. And ever since then, she won't leave their sides—or their backs, for that matter. Elvira loves to ride on the capys' backs, especially when the ground is wet or cold. Recently, after a big snow, Elvira wouldn't leave her spot, perched atop Cheesecake. "They don't have to be together, but they choose to be," says Janice of these quirky cuties. "Animals have no problem accepting each other's differences."

Capybaras can stay underwater for up to five minutes at a time.

PARROT FEEDS POOCH

LOCATION: SAN DIEGO, CALIFORNIA, U.S.A.

Motley Crue is a harlequin Great Dane, and though he is very large, he is as sweet and gentle as it gets. Need proof? His bestie is an eclectus parrot named Yoshi. Yoshi is constantly flying around the house, landing on Motley's head, and climbing all over him. "Motley is incredibly patient with Yoshi and never complains," says their owner, Amy Strickland. While Yoshi is still learning how to say "Motley Crue," one phrase he has down pat is "Good boy," which he says while Motley does tricks. Yoshi can also make kissing noises, which in the Strickland household can get a little confusing. "I'm not good at whistling, so the kissing noises have become the command for 'Come here,'" says Amy. "When Yoshi does it, it can get a little confusing for the poor dog." One perk that comes with having a parrot for a pal is getting to be the cleanup crew. Seeing as how birds are famously messy eaters, Motley stands and waits for any morsels Yoshi drops at breakfast. "Yoshi eats a homemade diet, and whenever he drops a noodle or bean, Motley is always there to clean up."

CAT GUARDS BEARDED DRAGON

LOCATION: WILMINGTON, DELAWARE, U.S.A.

It's always nice to have a friend who will stick up for you. That's exactly what Gerald the bearded dragon found in his pal Smokey the kitten. When Amy Stewart adopted Smokey for her son, James, and Gerald the bearded dragon for her daughter, Jacquelyne, they waited awhile before introducing Gerald to Smokey and the four other cats in the house. They wanted to be careful just in case the cats saw Gerald less as a sibling and more like a snack. But when Smokey finally got to have her first face-to-face with the little lizard, she was smitten. While she couldn't figure out exactly what Gerald was, she knew she liked him. Smokey has now become Gerald's personal bodyguard, putting herself between him and the other cats to make sure he's safe when they're around. Smokey curls up with the adorable reptile to keep him warm, and Gerald burrows beneath sweet Smokey's belly. The curious cat will playfully bat at Gerald's tail and will even happily scratch her face on his spikes. "Smokey even sits on top of Gerald's terrarium when he's not feeling social," says Amy. "They truly are adorable together."

GOAT JOINS DOG PACK

LOCATION: DAMME, BELGIUM

This goat may not bark, but he's still part of the dog pack! When Hans the goat was just three days old, Isolde Mattart brought him to live with her on her family's farm in Belgium. Hans's mother had passed away, and so Isolde adopted him, getting up multiple times each night to bottle-feed him. Right away, Isolde's two dogs, Basiel and Julie, took an interest in little Hans. Julie seemed to want to take care of Hans, while Basiel just wanted to play with him! Julie and Basiel taught Hans everything about how to get by on the farm, from leaving the ducks and chickens alone to avoiding the pond and not going near the street. Hans, who seems to think of himself as part of their pack, just copies their behavior. The three amigos nap together, go on long walks, cuddle, and sunbathe—Hans loves to sunbathe! The happy-go-lucky goat even jumps onto Julie's back and will ride around up there. Here's to the sweetest pack around!

BUNNY RACES TORTOISE

LOCATION: PORT ST. LUCIE, FLORIDA, U.S.A.

If you think you know the story of the tortoise and the hare, think again! Lola the rabbit and Stormo the tortoise are fast friends—well, Stormo's not too fast, but you get the point. These two love sharing treats, hiding under the couch together, and playing in the backyard. "Lola treats Stormo as if he were another bunny," says their owner, Jessica Grassi. "She will sprint ahead of Stormo, stop, look back at him, and wait for him to catch up. Since he is a bit of a slowpoke, sometimes she will run back to him, let him get ahead, then sprint forward again, and repeat." All that running around makes Stormo tuckered out; Jessica has found him catching some z's in all sorts of spots around the house. "He likes to find a nice, cozy corner to squeeze into," says Jessica. "He has been found under the TV stand, tucked in a corner in the kitchen, beneath a pile of clothes in the closet, under the bed, and on the bottom shelf of the bookcase."

LOLA

STORMO

Rabbits are born blind and without any fur. They live in a fur-lined nest for the first few days of their lives.

PIT BULL PINES FOR KITTY

LOCATION: LOS ANGELES, CALIFORNIA, U.S.A.

At the same time that Rebecca Pizzello rescued Bubba, a three-month-old pit bull puppy, her roommate was fostering a litter of kittens. That's all it took to turn sweet Bubba into a full-fledged cat lover. So a few years later when Rebecca adopted Rue, a seven-week-old kitten, Bubba was beside himself. "For the first few hours, Bubba would lay his head on my lap watching Rue climb all over me," says Rebecca. "He knew immediately how delicate she was and to be gentle." Rue would snuggle with Bubba and would often fall asleep on him. Bubba would lick Rue to bathe her and would always keep an eye out for her. In fact, all Rebecca would have to say is, "Go watch your sister," and Bubba would find Rue wherever she was. These two precious pals are attached at the hip and are rarely apart from each other—which is how they like it! When Rebecca started to notice that Rue seemed sad when Bubba would leave to go for a walk, she got Rue a special harness and leash. Now they all go on walks together!

BULL GETS GUARD GOOSE

LOCATION: WAIHIRERE, GISBORNE, NEW ZEALAND

A few days after Hamish, a highland bull, was born at the Eco Lodge in New Zealand, a white goose was found resting on his leg. Nobody knew where the goose came from, but since that day more than 10 years ago, the goose has hardly ever left Hamish's side. He seems to fancy himself Hamish's bodyguard. When a cow or another bull gets too close to Hamish, the brave bird will stretch out his neck, screech, and chase them away. Once, the lodge's owner tried moving Hamish to another rancher's pasture without the goose. Well, that didn't go so well! After one night apart, Hamish's feisty, feathered friend traveled all alone to find the bull in his new pasture. He may not be the bull in this friendship, but he's certainly bullheaded about being with his bud.

DOG RESCUES KANGAROO

LOCATION: VICTORIA, AUSTRALIA

Rex the German shorthaired pointer was out for a walk with his owner, Leonie Allan, in Australia when he started getting excited. Leonie thought maybe Rex had seen a snake nearby and so she tried to get him to stay by her side, but he was determined to investigate. He seemed to be interested in a kangaroo that had been hit by a car and, sadly, died on the side of the road. What Leonie didn't realize was that Rex had picked up on the scent of a baby inside the kangaroo's pouch—and it was alive! Rex picked up the baby roo in his mouth and gently placed it at Leonie's feet. While Leonie tried to figure out what to do, Rex doted on the joey, nuzzling him and playing with him and refusing to leave his side. Leonie and Rex brought the sweet little guy to Jirrahlinga Koala and Wildlife Sanctuary and named him Rex Jr. A few weeks later, Rex and Leonie went for a visit. The two friends immediately recognized each other and began to playfully lick and nudge one another. That's one friendship we won't forget.

Thanks to kangaroos' large back feet, they can travel nearly 30 feet (9 m) in a single jump.

THANKS FOR SAVING ME!

CAT CLAIMS CRITTERS

LOCATION: SÃO PAULO, BRAZIL

Cleo the cat is incredibly welcoming to all other animals—all other animals, that is, except other cats. "She likes to interact with lizards, dogs, frogs, and turtles," says Cleo's owner, André Costa, "but not with other cats. I don't understand why." Perhaps Cleo likes being queen of the kitty castle. A few years ago, this royal highness took in a new member of her court when a little owl fell out of his nest during a storm. Cleo welcomed him into their home with open paws. Right when Forbi the owl arrived, Cleo went over to him to check him out. She was calm, curious, and friendly. Still to this day, the two unlikely buds love to spend lots of time together snuggling. Cleo will even gently hold Forbi between her paws. Talk about trust! These two are incredibly sweet together and really enjoy each other's company. As André says, "We are a big, happy, unlikely family!"

PUP FINDS PERFECT PLAYMATES

LOCATION: HAYMARKET, VIRGINIA, U.S.A.

When rescue pup Bowie was first introduced to Kuzy and Moose, two baby Nigerian dwarf goats, they met through a fence to make sure they could get along. But Bowie wasn't interested in picking fights—all he wanted to do was play! He was beyond thrilled to have two new animals to pal around with outside. Sure, there were the occasional misunderstandings, like when the goats were convinced that Bowie was charging them. But now they know not to be scared when Bowie runs in their direction. And as for Bowie, he's had to get used to the funny, sideways way that the goats run (which has definitely led to a few near collisions). But the thing Bowie loves best of all is when the goats come inside the house. Since goats really do love eating almost anything and everything, it's not often that their owners—Susan Roberts and her dad, Larry—invite them in, but when they do, boy does Bowie think it's great! He romps around the kitchen trying to get them to play with him. Usually, though, the goats only have eyes for one thing inside the house: dryer lint, which they consider a rare and cherished snack!

CHEETAH'S BESTIE IS A DOG

ODIE

LOCATION: GREENWICH, CONNECTICUT, U.S.A.

Who says cats and dogs can't get along? Soon after the cheetah Adaeze was born, it became clear that his mother wasn't going to be able to take care of him. So keepers at the LEO Zoological Conservation Center in Connecticut stepped in to raise him. They wanted Adaeze to have a friend to play with, someone to keep him company, and maybe an animal who could help keep him calm. So they introduced him to an energetic Australian shepherd named Odie. The two got along wonderfully right from the start, and now they're the very best of friends. They love to play together, run around in the grass, wrestle, and play tug-of-war with toys. They also love to cuddle and sleep together, and whenever Adaeze takes part in presentations promoting cheetah preservation, Odie is there, right by his side. What a wild tale!

RESCUE DOG BECOMES KITTEN NANNY

LOCATION: PHOENIX, ARIZONA, U.S.A.

Boots, a sweet senior who was rescued after Hurricane Katrina, has found an extraordinary way to give back. He and his owner, Susan Juergensen, go once a week to the animal shelter where he works as a "kitten nanny"! If kittens have positive interactions with dogs when they're young, they'll be more likely to be comfortable around them as they get older. Plus, cats that are good with dogs have a better chance of being adopted. So Boots does his part to help! First he walks around the kittens' cages and sniffs them. If the kittens seem calm, curious, or excited and happy around Boots, they are slowly introduced and get to play. Boots lies down and the kittens are given the opportunity to approach him if they want to. Usually, the kittens climb all over sweet Boots, who is extremely patient and gentle with them. They meow at him, snuggle into his fur, and sometimes even lick his face. Boots seems to have found his (supercute) calling as a kitten nanny, and he couldn't be happier about it.

BOOTS

GOAT CALMS THOROUGHBRED

COASTER

LONELY LLAMA BEFRIENDS CHICKEN

LOCATION: ST. LOUIS, MISSOURI, U.S.A.

Fitting in to a new place—whether a school, or a farm!—can be tough. When Page Pardo brought Carll the llama to her farm, he had a hard time adjusting. He was used to being with other llamas, and here he was the only one. Page could tell he was lonely. So she brought in Evelyn, a chicken who had suffered an injury and needed a wheelchair. Right when Page brought Evelyn to Carll, he seemed happier. "Carll's demeanor immediately changed, and he was at ease," says Page. And the feeling was mutual. Evelyn, who was wary of other animals because of her injury, trusted Carll completely. In fact, when he put her beak in his mouth—something he does every time he sees her now—she closed her eyes and purred. "I was in awe," says Page. Evelyn, who didn't like other animals approaching her and definitely didn't like cuddles, wanted them from Carll. If Page puts Evelyn across the room from Carll, the determined little bird will scoot all the way over to him so that they can cuddle. "They both needed a friend," says Page. "Who knew a big, fuzzy llama would fit the bill for Evelyn, and a small, recovering hen in a wheelchair would be it for Carll?" No matter what, they're a perfect pair.

LOCATION: WOODINVILLE, WASHINGTON, U.S.A.

Coaster, a 13-year-old Thoroughbred horse, was having a tough time. He was anxious and unhappy and hated being left alone in his stall. His owner, Jennifer Sparks, and his trainers tried and tried to help lift his spirits, but nothing worked. That is, until a very smart groom thought to bring him a friend. And that friend was Buttercup, a little goat the groom had rescued. It took a little while for Coaster and Buttercup to get used to each other, but now that they have, they're best friends. The two buds make each other so happy that when Coaster travels to horse competitions, Buttercup goes, too. There is only one problem: When Coaster is out riding, Buttercup cries and calls to him until he returns! One thing Coaster and Buttercup have in common, aside from their love for each other, is that they both love gummy worms and banana-flavored candy. Now Coaster no longer hates being in his stall. In fact, at the barn where they live in Washington, they have a special stall made just for a horse and a goat!

FIERCE FRIENDS

These animals are powerful predators, but when it comes to their besties, they're all about the love. Read on for some of the wildest friendships you'll find!

LION, TIGER, AND BEAR ... OH MY!

LOCATION: LOCUST GROVE, GEORGIA, U.S.A.

What started as a very sad story for these three beauties had a very happy ending. At Noah's Ark wildlife rehabilitation center in Georgia, three amazing animals all lived together in one exhibit: Leo the African lion, Shere Khan the Bengal tiger, and Baloo the American black bear. While these are animals that would likely not peacefully coexist in the wild, they formed an unbreakable bond. The three sweeties were rescued by police officers from people who had illegally bought them as pets and were mistreating them. They were very sick and in need of medical help. Happily, the animals received the help and care they needed. But even after they were fed and exercised well, it became clear that they were happiest when they were all together. The gentle giants groomed and nuzzled one another, and they spent their days playing, running around, and relaxing. Sadly, Leo has since passed away, but Shere Khan and Baloo continue to be together. While they no doubt miss their brother, their friendship lives on.

Tigers are the largest members of the cat family.

WOLFDOG BEFRIENDS LITTLE DOG

LOCATION: LOS ANGELES, CALIFORNIA, U.S.A.

You can never be too tough to have a friend! When Paula Ficara and Steve Wastell rescued a wolfdog (a mix between a dog and a wolf) named Taboo, she was only a year old, hadn't been leash trained, and hadn't been exposed to other animals. "She was as wild as could be, flying around on the end of the leash like a kite," says Paula. Luckily, Paula and Steve are the founders of the Apex Protection Project (APP), a nonprofit organization that rescues captive-bred wolves and wolfdogs in need. It took many months of training and patience, but Taboo began to calm down. At first, Taboo was very scared of other dogs, but when a friend invited her to meet Eddie, their rescue Chihuahua/Jack Russell mix, Paula and Steve decided to give it a try. "We couldn't have been more pleasantly surprised," says Paula. Despite their differences, Taboo and Eddie were fast friends. The two chased each other and wrestled, and Taboo, who had seemed so wild at first, was very gentle with her much smaller pal. Today, Taboo is the leader of her own pack at the APP. She helps other rescued wolves and wolfdogs integrate into the pack and learn how to behave. But she will never forget her first friend, Eddie. As Paula says, "Taboo always looks forward to taking a break from the pack and having playtime with her bestie."

EDDIE
TABOO

WINSPEAR
AMANI

CHEETAH AND CANINE: WILD CAT ADVOCATES

LOCATION: DALLAS, TEXAS, U.S.A.

You might guess that big cats like cheetahs are naturally bold, but the truth is that these speedsters are often shy! Luckily for Winspear, a cheetah who lives at the Dallas Zoo, dogs have been found to be great companions for cheetahs. Dogs have warm, calm personalities that help cheetahs feel more comfortable and confident. That's definitely been the case for Winspear and Amani, his Labrador retriever pal. The two have lived together since they were six weeks old and, despite being different species, they have become like brothers! These days, the two animals travel together to participate in presentations about cheetahs and the threats they face in the wild. In these public settings, which can be stressful for shy cheetahs, Amani helps Winspear feel calmer and less anxious. Then, back at the zoo where they live together full-time, these BFFs play together, fetch balls, share toys, wrestle, give each other lots of kisses, and cuddle up when it's time to sleep.

CAT BECOMES ONE OF THE DOGS

LOCATION: WENTZVILLE, MISSOURI, U.S.A.

Kasey Boggs hadn't intended to get a cat. After all, she already had a dog. But after she moved into a house in the country that was infested with mice, she went to meet some rescue kittens in need of a home. Mia, a spunky little kitten with no tail, kept jumping on Kasey, trying to bite her ponytail. Kasey lifted the little ball of fur and looked her straight in the eyes, and right away she knew: She and Mia were meant to be together. Today, Mia has four dog siblings: Roxy, Edith, Rose, and Jake. But Mia doesn't mind palling around with pups, because she thinks of herself more like a dog than a cat! She likes to go on car rides, leads the pack when they all go for walks in the park, cuddles with the dogs, walks on a leash, and goes on long hikes (she rides in a special backpack that Kasey wears). All of Kasey's crew were rescued from very sad situations, but now, together, they have a happy life, a safe home, and, best of all, a family perfect for a canine-ish cat.

PIG CARES FOR INJURED GOAT

PINEY

ANGEL

LOCATION: ANNANDALE, NEW JERSEY, U.S.A.

Angel, a little goat who had lost both her ears and her back legs to frostbite, needed her own guardian angel. Luckily, Leanne Lauricella, a woman who started a goat rescue organization called the Goats of Anarchy™, took sweet Angel in. When Leanne brought Angel home, the little goat had a guardian angel waiting for her: a giant of a pig named Piney. Piney seemed to sense exactly what Angel needed. Piney would curl up with her in a large dog bed in front of the fire to comfort the injured goat and keep her warm. Thanks to Piney's constant care, Angel began to improve! Now she has a pink wheelchair cart so that she can move around on her own. But after her days of exploring, she still comes home to snuggle up with Piney.

CHICKEN AND CHIHUAHUA CHUMS

LOCATION: DULUTH, GEORGIA, U.S.A.

When Alicia Williams rescued a silkie chicken named Penny from a local animal-testing facility, she wasn't quite sure how to care for the beautiful bird. Luckily, Alicia works for an animal hospital in Georgia and the veterinarians there gave her some good advice: They said that since Penny is a flock animal, she needed to be around other animals. And in a twist of fate, shortly afterward someone brought in a special animal that would soon be Penny's pup. Little Roo, a Chihuahua with only two legs, was found in a ditch and in need of medical care as well as a loving home. Luckily, kind Alicia adopted Roo. When she introduced Roo to Penny, Roo playfully nibbled at Penny's feathers and the two rolled around together. When Roo got tuckered out and fell asleep, Penny perched on top of her like a mother hen over an egg! These days, this inspirational twosome spends all of their time together. Roo keeps up with Penny with the help of a special wheelchair, and the pals love to play outside, take baths, and eat together. They even visit hospitals, schools, and nursing homes to help brighten people's days.

ONE HAPPY FAMILY

GRETTA

MUK

WILLOW

SMUDGE

OLIVER

STORM

LOCATION: ALBERTA, CANADA

There's no shortage of animal friendships at Jody Jordan's farm, Pig~Tale Acres. Her crew of cuties includes Gretta, Smudge, and Muk (mini pigs); Khoopa (a sulcata tortoise); Storm and Cora (kittens); Mowgli, Cookie, and Daffy (ducklings); Jasper (a cat); Willow and Oliver (Yorkies); Tinkerbell (a border collie); and Katy (a bearded dragon)! Muk was bullied by his former littermates, but once he realized Smudge was a sweetie, the two have been best friends ever since. Khoopa and Storm were adopted from a farm rescue together because they'd become besties there and Jody didn't want to separate them. Storm was super comfortable with pigs from living at the farm, so when he got to Jody's, he and Smudge became fast friends. Storm would even ride around on Smudge's back while he grazed around the yard. The three ducks were abandoned, and when Jody took them in, they too became attached to the pigs. She would often find them sleeping right on top of Smudge and Muk. "At any time, I can look out my kitchen window and enjoy the many friendships that exist among our pets," says Jody. "We are very lucky to have so many animals that get along."

Pigs have poor eyesight but a great sense of smell.

RABBIT AND CAT: PARTNERS IN CRIME

LOCATION: NASHVILLE, TENNESSEE, U.S.A.

When Katja Russell and her husband, Nick, brought home an Angora rabbit named Barnaby, it took some adjusting for Butler, their rescued Manx cat. No one could have guessed that the pair would eventually become a rascally duo! The introduction between the two cuties started off fine, but then Barnaby did what's called a "bunny binky," a happy little bunny hop, and Butler got scared. Barnaby seemed to pick up on Butler's dislike for his hopping and started trying to crawl to be more like Barnaby! While watching this beautiful bunny crawl like a cat was cute, Katja and Nick wanted to make sure Barnaby felt comfortable being himself. So they encouraged him to hop and bounce, and pretty soon Butler got used to his silly new friend. Now these two have become precious partners in crime! They bird-watch together, they play with cat toys together, they share laps together (if one is being petted, the other jumps on top to get pets, too), and they even steal treats together. In fact, more than once Katja has gotten up in the middle of the night to find one knocking treats off the table for the other. Katja says, "It was so funny, I couldn't get mad."

LOCATION: EHRINGHAUSEN, GERMANY

When the Dahlhaus family found Manni, a wild boar, abandoned in a field, he was only a few weeks old and hadn't eaten in quite a while. He was in bad shape. So the kind family took him into their home in Germany and nursed him back to health. Bottle-feeding Manni helped fill his belly, but the precious piglet was still frightened and lonely. To lift his spirits, the Dahlhaus family introduced Manni to their family pet, a Jack Russell terrier named Candy. The two became the best of buds. They bounded around the yard together, running, jumping, and playing hide-and-seek. Manni was so smitten with his new bud that he even began trying to bark just like a dog! But barks or oinks, these pals are speaking the language of friendship.

MANNI

CANDY

WILD BOAR FINDS PUP PLAYMATE

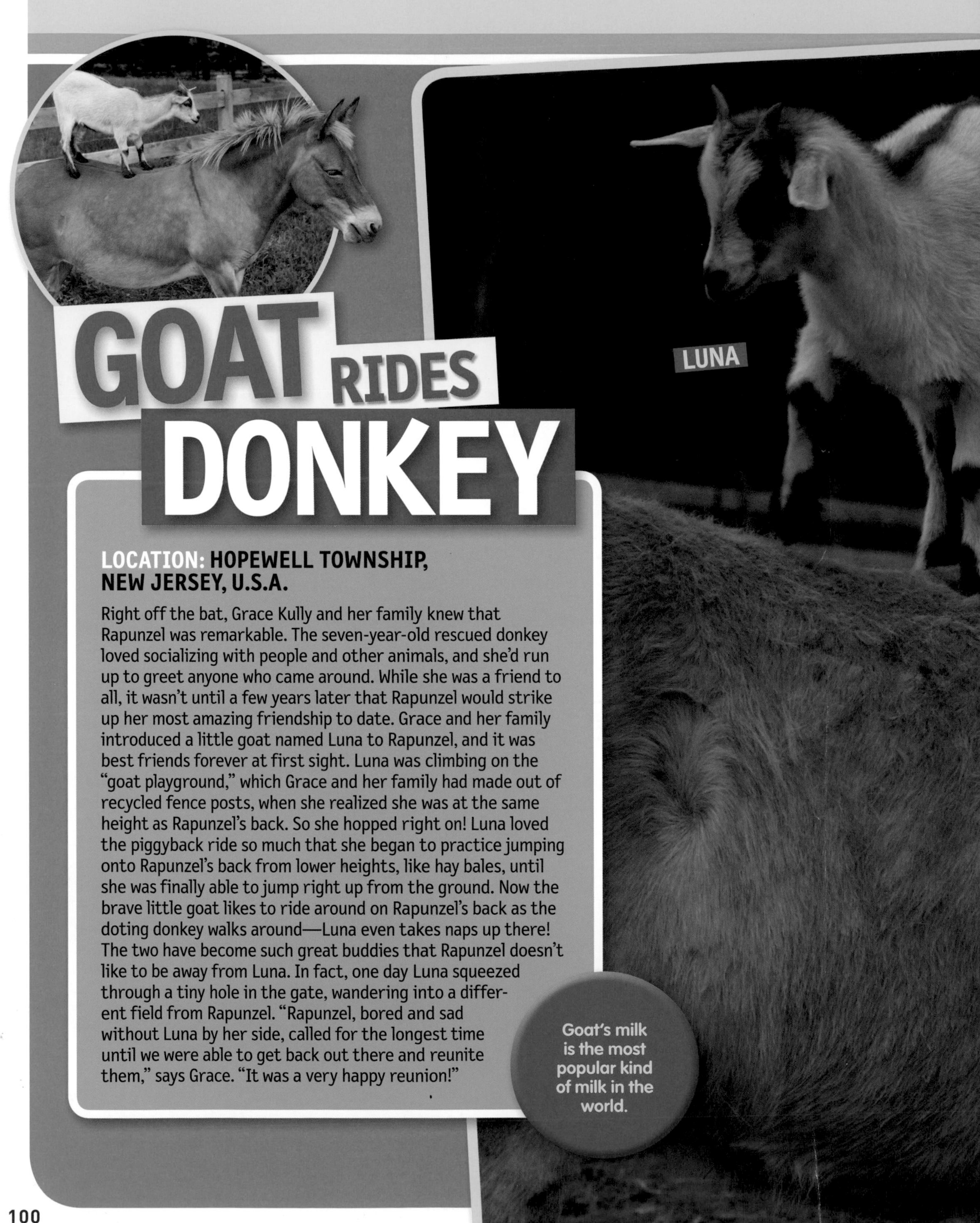

GOAT RIDES DONKEY

LOCATION: HOPEWELL TOWNSHIP, NEW JERSEY, U.S.A.

Right off the bat, Grace Kully and her family knew that Rapunzel was remarkable. The seven-year-old rescued donkey loved socializing with people and other animals, and she'd run up to greet anyone who came around. While she was a friend to all, it wasn't until a few years later that Rapunzel would strike up her most amazing friendship to date. Grace and her family introduced a little goat named Luna to Rapunzel, and it was best friends forever at first sight. Luna was climbing on the "goat playground," which Grace and her family had made out of recycled fence posts, when she realized she was at the same height as Rapunzel's back. So she hopped right on! Luna loved the piggyback ride so much that she began to practice jumping onto Rapunzel's back from lower heights, like hay bales, until she was finally able to jump right up from the ground. Now the brave little goat likes to ride around on Rapunzel's back as the doting donkey walks around—Luna even takes naps up there! The two have become such great buddies that Rapunzel doesn't like to be away from Luna. In fact, one day Luna squeezed through a tiny hole in the gate, wandering into a different field from Rapunzel. "Rapunzel, bored and sad without Luna by her side, called for the longest time until we were able to get back out there and reunite them," says Grace. "It was a very happy reunion!"

Goat's milk is the most popular kind of milk in the world.

I SHOULD START CHARGING FOR THIS.
RAPUNZEL

FAWN FINDS FRIEND IN RESCUED RABBIT

LOCATION: BUFFALO, NEW YORK, U.S.A.

When Leondra Scherer, a wildlife rescuer and rehabilitator, got a call in mid-September that there was a fawn in need of her help, she thought it must be a mistake. Baby deer are typically born between May and August in upstate New York, and it would be very rare for one to be born so late in the season. But sure enough, what Leondra found was an orphaned one-day-old fawn in desperate need of some help. Leondra named her Pumpkin and brought her home to care for her. It's important for fawns to have an animal companion they can interact with, but all of the other fawns Leondra had rehabilitated were much older than Pumpkin and were getting ready to be released back into the wild. So Leondra decided to look elsewhere for a pal for Pumpkin. She went to the SPCA and adopted Chunk, a super laid-back rabbit. "At this point, I wasn't sure if it would work," says Leondra about her matchmaking attempts. But when she put Chunk down near Pumpkin, he immediately hopped over to her and they snuggled up together to take a nap. And that's all it took—they were fast friends. From that point on they spent their days together snuggling and playing. "If you see a picture of Pumpkin and you can't see Chunk," says Leondra, "he's there, he's just burrowed beneath her." Awww! The snuggle is real!

OWL SNUGGLES DOG

LOCATION: BROWNS VALLEY, CALIFORNIA, U.S.A.

When Louise, a baby Eurasian eagle owl, arrived at master falconer Jim Tigan's home, she had traveled by plane across the country and was thirsty and a little out of sorts. Jim and his wife, Kathleen, gave her water, got her warmed up, and made her a comfy nest out of pillows and blankets on the couch. But the next morning when they woke up, Louise wasn't on the couch. They looked all over the house for the baby bird. When they finally found her, she was curled up with their dog, a wirehaired pointing griffon named Annabelle. From that point on, says Jim, "Louise just always wanted to be around Annabelle." Once, Annabelle fell asleep in the backyard with a squeaky toy in her mouth and Louise snuck up to her and stole it. The two had the best time, chasing each other around the backyard, trying to get the toy. Then the surprising pair took the Internet by storm when Jim posted a video of Louise gently preening Annie with her claws and beak. The patient dog can be seen sitting calmly while the owl pets her with her large talons. These two have a "one-in-a-million" bond.

DOG BECOMES CARETAKER

LOCATION: VICTORIA, AUSTRALIA

Eileen, an Irish wolfhound, is an exceptional dog with a heart of gold. After she was rescued from a bad situation, she was brought to live at the Cremona Hillside farm in Australia with Kate and Alex Serrurier. There, she has become a mother figure to other sick or orphaned animals. Whenever Kate and Alex present Eileen with a new animal that needs her help, the big dog will immediately begin licking it to get the animal's heartbeat up, just like a mother sheep would. She warms the animal and licks its face to encourage it to start eating. One such animal, Valiant, was a little lamb who wouldn't nurse from his mother. Eileen was more than happy to step in and help, snuggling Valiant and giving him loads of love and attention. Now Valiant is healthy and happy! Eileen is beloved by all of the animals on the farm—lambs, goats, kittens. Even human babies love her. "The other day I noticed that my one-year-old grandson seemed to have his hair done very nicely," says Kate. "Then suddenly I realized that Eileen had also groomed him and done his hair. He even had a part!"

Irish wolfhounds have rough coats that keep them warm in cold, damp weather.

LIFE WOULD BE RUFF WITHOUT FRIENDS.

SUZIE AND HER FOSTER KITTENS

Page 60

BUT WITH YOU IT'S PAWS-ITIVELY AWESOME!

YOU'VE GOT A FRIEND IN ME!

Beth and Lion Cub
Page 70

It's pretty amazing how animals can look past big differences to form friendships that last a lifetime. To the animals in this book, it didn't matter their buddy's size, speed, or even species. The only criterion these critters cared about is whether or not their friend was a good one!

Chompers and Littlefoot
Pages 52–53

So, what makes a good friend? Here are 10 tips for being the best bud you can be!

Lulú and Moonlight
Page 79

1. **Respect each other's differences.** Life would be pretty boring if we were all the same. Give your friends the space and support they need to be their awesome and unique selves!
2. **Listen.** Everybody wants to feel like their thoughts and ideas matter. A great way to show someone that you care about what they have to say is by really listening when they speak. Try not to interrupt or change the subject, and instead give lots of good eye contact and some supportive head nods.
3. **Don't make a big deal out of little things.** In other words, ditch the drama. Focus on the things that really matter and let the small stuff go.
4. **Find common ground.** Whether it's basketball, baking, or botany, find things you like to do together and subjects you like to talk about.
5. **Don't gossip or talk behind each other's backs.** Yep, just don't do it.
6. **Give each other space.** When you start to get on each other's nerves, it doesn't mean your friendship's doomed, it just means you might need to step away, take a break, and do your own thing for a bit.
7. **Learn how to disagree respectfully.** It's cool to have friends with different beliefs, ideas, and opinions. That's how you become a more interesting person. But, to make sure no one's feelings get hurt, learn how to express yourself without disrespecting someone else.
8. **Keep in touch!** Some people prefer email; others only want to text. Figure out the best way for you and your friends to chat even when you're apart.
9. **Show up during hard times!** If you don't know the right thing to say when someone you care about is going through a hard time, don't let that keep you from saying anything at all. It's okay to be awkward, it's okay to be uncomfortable—but show up anyway.
10. **Laugh a lot and have FUN!** Enjoy each other and make loads of memories.

Penny and Little Roo
Page 97

Rex and Rex Jr.
Pages 88–89

Index

Boldface indicates illustrations.

Index

Credits

FRONT COVER: (Spanky & Dally), Isobel Springett; (Mercy & Ella), Anna Davis-Key; (Emmett & Cullen), Grahm S. Jones, Columbus Zoo and Aquarium; (Jet & Miri), Nathan Edwards/Newspix/REX; **SPINE:** Isobel Springett; **BACK COVER** (LE), Tamala Lester, The Barnyard Sanctuary; (UP RT), Leslie Unruh, A to Z Alpacas; (LO CTR), Lehigh Valley Zoo; (LO RT), Natasha Stirk

INTERIOR: 1, Ann Bryant; 2-3, Hope Hall, Sunflower Farm Creamery; 4 (UP LE), Tamala Lester, The Barnyard Sanctuary; 4 (CTR), Nathan Edwards/Newspix/REX; 4 (LO RT), Leanne Lauricella, Goats of Anarchy, Inc.; 5 (UP LE), Kelly Hartman; 5 (CTR), Ileana M. Cotes S., Science Educator and Conservationist, Colegio Brader Middle School Principal, Panama; 5 (LO RT), Amy Strickland; 6 (UP), National Geographic Channel; 6 (CTR), Jody Jordan;6 (LO), Alissa Kampert; 7 (ALL), Tamala Lester, The Barnyard Sanctuary; 8-9, Nathan Edwards/Newspix/REX; 10 (ALL), National Geographic Channel; 11 (UP RT), Crystalyn Falk Corso; 11 (LO LE), Jackie and Paul Barbush; 12 (ALL), National Geographic Channel; 13 (UP RT), National Geographic Channel; 13 (LO LE), Ashley DiFelice; 14 (UP RT), Denise DiForio; 14 (LO LE), Ashley DeFelice; 15, Talitha Girnus; 16-17 (ALL), Hope Hall, Sunflower Farm Creamery; 18 (UP), Torgeir Berge; 18 (LO), Perla Rodriguez; 19 (ALL), Tanja Brandt; 20, Grahm S. Jones, Columbus Zoo and Aquarium; 21 (UP LE BOTH), Page Pardo; 21 (LO RT BOTH), National Geographic Channel; 22 (ALL), Jim and Jenny Desmond; 23 (UP LE BOTH), Jacquie Litton; 23 (LO RT), National Geographic Channel; 24 (ALL), Richard Austin; 25 (LE BOTH), Ben Beade/ Australia Zoo; 25 (UP RT), National Geographic Channel; 26 (UP LE), Mikael Buck/solentnews.biz; 26 (CTR), Abby Flynn; 26-27, Abby Flynn; 27 (UP LE), Leslie Unruh, A to Z Alpacas; 27 (CTR LE), Abby Flynn; 27 (LO LE), Abby Flynn; 28-29 (ALL), Nathan Edwards/Newspix/REX; 30 (ALL), Farm Animal Rescue of Mifflinburg; 31 (UP RT), National Geographic Channel; 31 (LO LE), Allison Hedgecoth, Noah's Ark Animal Sanctuary; 32 (UP LE), Lehigh Valley Zoo; 32 (LO RT), Taylor Williams; 33, Leanne Lauricella, Goats of Anarchy, Inc.; 34-35 (ALL), Tamala Lester, The Barnyard Sanctuary; 36, Natasha Stirk; 37 (UP LE), National Geographic Channel; 37 (LO RT), Farm Sanctuary; 38-39, Mikhail Soldatenkov, Leningrad Zoo; 38 (UP LE), Mikhail Soldatenkov, Leningrad Zoo; 38 (LO LE), Janice Wolf; 39 (UP CTR), Mikhail Soldatenkov, Leningrad Zoo; 39 (LO RT), Tessa Reber; 40-41 (ALL), Isobel Springett; 42 (UP RT), Kristy Gamayo; 42 (LO LE), Ann Bryant; 43 (ALL), Leslie Unruh, A to Z Alpacas; 44, AP Photo/Erie Times-News, Greg Wohlford; 45 (UP RT), Christina Cross; 45 (LO LE), Farm Sanctuary; 46, Dan Callister, PacificCoastNews/Newscom; 47 (UP LE), Tara Rex; 47 (LO RT), Lori Epstein/ National Geographic Creative; 48 (ALL), Taneile Hoare; 49 (UP RT), Victoria Trovato; 49 (LO LE), Caitlin Cimini; 50 (UP LE), National Geographic Channel; 50 (LO RT), Jordan Russo, Farm Animal Refuge; 51 (ALL), Pam Ahern; 52-53 (ALL), Alissa Kampert; 54, National Geographic Channel; 55 (UP RT), National Geographic Channel; 55 (LO LE), Teresa Tuffi; 56 (UP LE), Kendall Smith; 56 (LO RT), Barbara Jamison; 57, Anna Davis-Key; 58-59, White House Photo/Alamy Stock Photo; 58 (LO LE), Zoo Atlanta; 59 (UP LE), Pete Souza/The White House/Getty Images; 59 (LO LE), Sebastian Smetham; 60 (UP BOTH), Kelly Hartman; 60 (LO RT), Alison Otter; 61 (ALL), National Geographic Channel; 62, Rupa Sutton; 63 (UP LE), National Geographic Channel; 63 (LO RT), Lindley Beckman Turner; 64-65 (ALL), Alex DeForest, Arizona Humane Society; 66 (UP RT), National Geographic Channel; 66 (LO LE), Leanne Lauricella, Goats of Anarchy, Inc.; 67 (ALL), National Geographic Channel; 68 (ALL), Loraine De Souza Winterstail; 69 (UP RT), Save the Chimps; 69 (LO LE), National Geographic Channel; 70 (ALL), Wesley Wallace; 71 (UP RT), National Geographic Channel; 71 (LO LE), Lindley Beckman Turner; 72 (UP LE), Washington Department of Fish & Wildlife; 72-73, Page Pardo; 73 (UP RT), Lorrie Anzalone; 73 (CTR), Page Pardo; 74 (UP), Photograph copyright 2006 by Peter Greste; 74 (LO), Thomas Omondi/ REX/Shutterstock; 75 (UP RT), Shelby Madere; 75 (LO LE), National Geographic Channel; 76-77 (ALL), Hoedspruit Endangered Species Centre (HESC); 78 (ALL), Richard Austin; 79 (UP RT), Ileana Cotes; 79 (LO LE), Kristin Hooper; 80, National Geographic Channel; 81 (UP RT), Lindley Beckman Turner; 81 (LO LE), Thi Bui; 82, Edward Tate; 83 (UP LE), National Geographic Channel; 83 (LO RT), Janice Wolf, Rocky Ridge Refuge; 84 (LE), Amy Strickland; 85 (UP LE BOTH), Amy L. Stewart; 85 (RT BOTH), Isolde Mattart; 86 (UP RT), Jess Grassi; 86 (LO LE), Rebecca Pizzello; 87, Gisborne Herald; 88-89 (ALL), Newspix/REX/Shutterstock; 90 (ALL), André Costa Biologist - São Caetano do Sul/São Paulo - Brazil; 91 (UP RT), Lori Epstein/National Geographic Creative; 91 (LO LE), LEO Zoological Conservation Center; 92 (UP LE), National Geographic Channel; 92-93, Leah Raphael; 93 (CTR RT), Page Pardo; 94, Allison Hedgecoth, Noah's Ark Animal Sanctuary; 95 (UP RT), Paula Ficara, Apex Protection Project; 95 (LO LE), Cathy Burkey, Dallas Zoo; 96 (UP RT), Kasey Boggs; 96 (LO LE), Leanne Lauricella, Goats of Anarchy; 97, Alicia Williams; 98 (ALL), Jody Jordan; 99 (UP LE), Katja Russell; 99 (LO RT), Sascha Schuermann/ AFP/Getty Images; 100-101 (ALL), Mary Beth Kully and Grace Kully; 102 (ALL), Leondra Schere; 103 (UP RT), Kate and Alex Serrurier, Cremona Hillside Farm; 103 (LO LE), National Geographic Channel; 104-105, Kelly Hartman; 106 (UP), Wesley Wallace; 106 (LO RT), Alissa Kampert; 107 (UP RT), Ileana Cotes; 107 (CTR RT), Alicia Williams, Duluth Animal Hospital; 107 (LO RT), Newspix/REX/Shutterstock; 112, Sascha Schuermann/AFP/Getty Images

Since 1888, the National Geographic Society has funded more than 12,000 research, exploration, and preservation projects around the world. The Society receives funds from National Geographic Partners, LLC, funded in part by your purchase. A portion of the proceeds from this book supports this vital work. To learn more, visit natgeo.com/info.

For more information, visit nationalgeographic.com, call 1-800-647-5463, or write to the following address:

National Geographic Partners
1145 17th Street N.W.
Washington, D.C. 20036-4688 U.S.A.

Visit us online at nationalgeographic.com/books

For librarians and teachers: ngchildrensbooks.org

More for kids from National Geographic: natgeokids.com

For information about special discounts for bulk purchases, please contact National Geographic Books Special Sales: specialsales@natgeo.com

For rights or permissions inquiries, please contact National Geographic Books Subsidiary Rights: bookrights@natgeo.com

Designed by Ashita.Design

National Geographic supports K–12 educators with ELA Common Core Resources. Visit natgeoed.org/commoncore for more information.

Library of Congress Cataloging-in-Publication Data

Names: Gerry, Lisa, author. | National Geographic Society (U.S.)
Title: 125 animal friendships / by Lisa M. Gerry.
Other titles: One hundred and twenty-five animal friendships | National Geographic kids.
Description: Washington, DC : National Geographic Kids, [2018] | Audience: Ages 8-12. | Audience: Grades 4 to 6.
Identifiers: LCCN 2017035086| ISBN 9781426330186 (pbk.) | ISBN 9781426330193 (hardcover)
Subjects: LCSH: Animal behavior--Anecdotes--Juvenile literature. | Social behavior in animals--Anecdotes--Juvenile literature. | Animals--Miscellanea--Juvenile literature.
Classification: LCC QL751.5 .G47 2018 | DDC 591.5--dc23
LC record available at https://lccn.loc.gov/2017035086

The publisher would like to thank: Lisa M. Gerry, author; Roberta Lenarz, project manager; Liz Seramur, photo editor; Paige Towler, project editor; Sanjida Rashid, art director; Lori Epstein, photo director; Jennifer Kelly Geddes, fact-checker; Alix Inchausti, production editor; and Anne LeongSon and Gus Tello, production assistants.

Printed in China
18/RRDS/1

Manni and Candy
Page 99